the BOOKROOM

I0803957

"The weight of our imperfect history lies heavy upon us. Remembrance is necessary, but so, too, is forgiveness. We cannot live without both, and they cannot exist for long apart from each other."

—Wilfred McClay

"This moving memoir is two stories in one. It is a young boy's emotional journey from an isolated island through a desert to embrace the Trinitarian dance of love. It is also a scholar's journey in building a bridge from that island to the mainland in a way that both appreciates the restorationist impulse and the value of the Great Tradition. The two journeys—emotional and intellectual—are intertwined. One shapes the other to produce a compassionate maturity that centers itself in God's Triune relationality. Told with emotional depth and filled with grateful appreciation yet sober reflection, Leonard offers insight into each of our own journeys as we enter his."

—**John Mark Hicks,** author of *Meeting God at* The Shack*: A Journey into Spiritual Recovery*

"I thought I would read a little and ended up reading the whole thing in one sitting—which means this is a great read. Leonard Allen writes with a candor schooled by a life made possible by a faith that demands truth. He is serious but entertaining. We are fortunate to have the witness of one whose life is inseparable from a church he loves critically."

—**Stanley Hauerwas,** Duke University; author of *Hannah's Child: A Theological Memoir*

"Most theology is autobiography, as Frederick Buechner once noted. In this compelling memoir, Leonard Allen reveals the shaping of at least three theological trajectories. He shares the resources, both fertile and desolate, that formed his own remarkable life. He weaves stories from his particular faith tradition, which he, as much as any single person, has helped transform. And for those who can see it, he provides insights into the shaping of all our lives by modeling both the power of remembering and the courage of forgiveness."

—**Jack Reese,** author of *At the Blue Hole: An Elegy for a Church on the Edge*

"*The Bookroom* tells the powerful story of a journey toward a faith that builds bridges instead of walls. In this captivating memoir, Leonard Allen travels a path through the strict religious practices of his austere father into a long quest for understanding. The voice is so strong and the detail so rich that I was pulled into the place and time—just gorgeous writing. But it is more than one man's story. It's a story inviting us all to reconsider our own assumptions and to embark on our own journey toward a richer, more expansive faith."

—**Dana Chamblee Carpenter,** author of the *Bohemian Trilogy*

"Leonard Allen's moving memoir weaves together personal experience, theological reflection, and spiritual pilgrimage. In deeply personal terms he reminds us that to ignore our history, individual and communal, is to fail to fully understand ourselves. It's a splendid recounting of his journey and a welcome companion on ours. It makes for deeply engaging reading."

—**Randy Harris,** author of *Living Jesus: Doing What Jesus Says in the Sermon on the Mount*

"Leonard Allen has devoted his career to enhancing our understanding of the restoration movement, its history and its place in the great stream of Christianity. In *The Bookroom*, he has given us a wonderfully moving, personal account that displays the richness and depth of the Christian faith, the restoration and reconciliation we experience in Christ, and the good available to us in his church."

—**Candice McQueen,** President, Lipscomb University

"'Writing is easy,' sportswriter Red Smith once said. 'Just open a vein and bleed it out drop by drop.' In these brilliantly written vignettes, Leonard Allen candidly drops his lifeblood on the page. His reflections on growing up Church of Christ with an enquiring mind resonate with many of us. By engaging with this memoir, we will be led, like him, to both appreciate and forgive the heritage given to us by our physical and spiritual fathers and mothers. Through it we may also be able to receive the beauty of our Spirit-filled tradition."

—**Gary Holloway,** coauthor of *Renewing God's People: A Concise History of Churches of Christ*

"Leonard Allen continues his insightful writing about the history and theology of the Stone–Campbell Restoration Movement. Only this time it takes the form of a very creative memoir. The driving theme is his relentless search for answers to the perplexing theological questions growing out of his childhood experiences. It is all there—the good times and the bad and everything in between. Readers who have grown up in a similar heritage will relate immediately to the struggles of his journey."

—**Royce Money,** President Emeritus, Abilene Christian University

"As Leonard Allen acknowledges, our theology, practice of faith, and personal spiritual formation are shaped—more than we often know—by where we have come from and the people who have influenced us. Reading *The Bookroom* likely will do for you what it has for me. The prompts of his experiences will trigger a fresh exploration of your own spiritual life and placement in the Body of Christ. This vulnerable memoir from a respected scholar is both an education and a journey to share."

—**Rubel Shelly,** author of *I Knew Jesus before He Was a Christian—And I Liked Him Better Then*

the BOOKROOM

Remembrance and Forgiveness

A MEMOIR

C. Leonard Allen

Abilene Christian University Press

THE BOOKROOM

Remembrance and Forgiveness—A Memoir

ACU PRESS

Copyright © 2024 by C. Leonard Allen

ISBN 978-1-68426-043-0

Printed in the United States of America

ALL RIGHTS RESERVED
No part of this publication may be reproduced, stored in a retrieval system, or transmitted in any form by any means—electronic, mechanical, photocopying, recording, or otherwise—without prior written consent.

Scripture quotations are taken from the Holy Bible, New International Version®, NIV®. Copyright ©1973, 1978, 1984, 2011 by Biblica, Inc.™ Used by permission of Zondervan. All rights reserved worldwide.

Cataloging-in-Publication Data is on file at the Library of Congress, Washington, DC.

Cover design by Greg Jackson, Thinkpen Design
Interior text design by Sandy Armstrong, Strong Design

For information contact:
Abilene Christian University Press
ACU Box 29138
Abilene, Texas 79699

1-877-816-4455
www.acupressbooks.com

24 25 26 27 28 29 30 // 7 6 5 4 3 2 1

To Holly

and our children,

David, Daniel, and Bethany

CONTENTS

PREFACE

I never thought I would write a book like this one. It began when my daughter, Bethany, who works as a journalist, asked me to write stories about my life. Not only did she ask me; she gave me—graciously, of course—a timetable in which to do it. Once I got started, to my surprise, the stories kept coming, though not always on schedule. When I would miss a couple of weeks, Bethany would text me: "When is the next story coming, Dad?" So I would get back to it and soon have another story to send her. This collection does not contain all the stories, just the ones I thought could make up a coherent and perhaps artful whole.

This is not an autobiography. It doesn't aim to tell a whole life story. Rather, it is a memoir. It focuses on a pivotal season in my childhood when I began forming a cluster of questions about my family's church and the faith I inherited. Those questions, in time, gave rise to a life project, and it is that project that the following stories unfold.

My childhood church was the Churches of Christ. This Christian stream originated in the United States in the early nineteenth century. Two Scots-Irish Presbyterians, Barton Stone and Alexander Campbell, thought a simpler Christian faith—free of the strictures of human-made creeds—would bring unity and vitality. Stone was in Kentucky; Campbell in West Virginia. Their two unity movements united in 1832 and were variously called Christian Churches, Disciples of Christ, and Churches of Christ.

By the late nineteenth century, this unity movement had divided—as unity movements tend to do. There were the more rural, Southern, and conservative Churches of Christ and the more urban, Northern, and progressive Disciples of Christ. There were a few strong doctrinal disagreements, to be sure. But mainly the division resulted from sectional and social tensions below the surface of things.

Through the later-twentieth century, Churches of Christ experienced steady growth. By the opening of the twenty-first century, they numbered approximately 1.5 million adherents in over twelve thousand congregations in North America, with more than double that number of members in churches outside the United States.

In my vocation as a theologian, I sought primarily to address this lively—and often cantankerous—Christian tradition. Though beginning as a unity movement, it had eventually adopted—ironically—a strong separatist posture toward other Christians. I have described this development as moving to an island. My work over four decades primarily has been about building a bridge back to the mainland. It has been about understanding and connecting with the larger Christian story.

This memoir shows how personal—and how necessary—this work was to me, what its fruit has been, and where I have come out. Along the way, I employ five metaphors to help tell the story: (1) gathering around a table—a childhood dinner table, followed by two other quite different tables; (2) living in a desert—a dangerous desert of the heart and spirit; (3) climbing a mountain—but not your run-of-the-mill mountain; (4) learning to dance—not the Texas two-step but a dance far more lovely; and (5) crossing a long bridge—a passage to larger Christian regions.

I think most readers will identify with some or perhaps many of these stories. You will recognize some of the characters; you will smile, laugh, and feel some of the grief along the way. And in these stories you will get glimpses into the varied texture of our lives—the place of memory, the influence of tradition, the desert experiences, the need for forgiveness, the gifts along the way, the surprises of grace. And I think you will see that the Christian faith is richer and broader than we have often thought.

CHAPTER 1

THE BOOKROOM

> "Human persons become more rather than less mysterious the better we know them."
>
> —Eugene F. Rogers Jr.

The bookroom was the most mysterious room in my childhood home. It was my father's bedroom, office, and library. I first remember it as an upstairs room in our big two-story house outside Florence, Alabama, when I was five years old. But my main memory of it was in our small three-bedroom stucco house in Central Florida beginning at age seven.

A four-poster double bed occupied much of the room. Next to the bed was a large metal desk and a four-drawer filing cabinet. I can still see it clearly: the stacks of papers lying about the desk, the open books laid around the room, and the rows of mostly drab-looking books artfully balanced on rickety shelves. There was the distinctive—not entirely unpleasant—smell I later described as a dusty book smell tinctured by the faint scent of sweat from his gardening clothes. The whole aura of the room remains vividly imprinted in my memory, more vividly in fact than those wonderfully exciting biographies of George Washington Carver, Abraham Lincoln, and a dozen others I read during those elementary school years.

I thought of it as the bookroom. I was a frequent visitor—sometimes welcome, sometimes not. There was more than a hint of mystery and awe in that room, especially when I slipped in alone, sat in my father's chair (it swiveled), and tried to imagine what high and holy things transpired there between my father the professor and preacher and all those silent, ever-present books. Whatever it was, I promised myself, one day I would find out.

Most of the books were black hardbacks with no dust jackets. They looked old. Some were dusty. These, I soon learned, were all books about the Bible and our church. There were some colorful paperbacks on a couple of shelves, and these were all about gardening and how to be healthy. At one end were several stacks of magazines: *Progressive Farmer*, *Prevention*, *Gospel Advocate*, and a little pocket-sized one called *Sunshine* (the inside front cover said: "A little magazine of uplifting stories and anecdotes to cheer people up").

My father spent a lot of time in this room. Most of the time, it seemed to me, he was resting on the bed, usually reading. Sometimes he was sitting at the big desk writing. On one wall was a framed drawing of a stallion in charcoal or pen. On the wall over the desk, also framed, was a Bible verse spelled out in brown, hand-painted block letters: "Whatever you do, in word or deed, do it all to the glory of God." He had created both pieces many years before.

The room was a mystery to me because my father was a mystery to me. What was he about? Where did his way of being come from? What did all these books have to do with it? I was seven, maybe eight, when the mystery of this room—of him—drew me in. What clues could it give me? What clues could he? I found myself slipping into the bookroom alone. I was not afraid of being caught. I just wanted to figure some things out.

Sometimes I would sit on the floor at the foot of the bed and pull out several black hardbacks. For example, a book with the puzzling title *Larimore and His Boys* (1889) by F. B. Srygley. Or another very large tome with the strange title *The Hardeman-Bogard Debate* by N. B. Hardeman and Ben M. Bogard (1938). Or a seven-hundred-page volume titled *Questions Answered* (1921) by David Lipscomb and E. G. Sewell. I didn't read much in them, but I sometimes asked my father questions about them later when he was lying on the bed.

"Who was T. B. Larimore, and what is this book about?" I asked. And he replied, "Larimore was a well-known gospel preacher who died about forty years ago. When we lived in Florence and you attended Mars Hill Bible School in first grade, his homeplace was on that property. And he started that school."

And I followed up by asking, "What is a debate, and why did Mr. Hardeman and Mr. Bogard have one?" And he said, "A debate is a public argument where two people take different sides of an issue. Bogard was a Baptist minister, and Hardeman represented the Church of Christ." He added, "Debates have been a common way of upholding God's truth against error."

That seemed strange to me. But I was glad to know about it. Mr. Lipscomb's big book seemed more straightforward: hundreds of questions about the Bible from readers of his magazine, the *Gospel Advocate*. I perused the questions and attempted to read a few. "Is one church as good as another?" someone asked. The answer, I could tell, was a resounding "No!" But the long and dense response was mostly beyond me. Another wanted to know, "Is the church of Christ a denomination in the common acceptation of the term?" Again, the answer was "No!" with a long explanation. These were topics, I would soon learn, that would be a strong part of my early indoctrination—in the bookroom and around the dinner table.

Over the years that followed, the big Lipscomb book would provide some important clues to the mystery of my father. I will get to that in several later stories.

Gardening and good health were the two other main themes of the bookroom. On health, the author who stood out was Adelle Davis, who was big in the 1960s and 1970s. The two books I saw on the shelves, which I heard my parents talk about regularly, were *Let's Get Well: A Practical Guide to Renewed Health Through Nutrition* (1965) and *Let's Eat Right to Keep Fit* (1954). Davis praised the value of natural foods and sharply criticized the diet of the average American, which she argued was excessively high in salt, refined sugars, preservatives, and other additives. This was long before the time of Whole Foods Market and the natural foods movement.

The other food guru my parents talked about was J. I. Rodale, an early advocate of sustainable agriculture and organic farming in the United States. And through his magazine *Prevention* (1950), he promoted—like Davis—a return to whole grains, unrefined sweets, using minimal saturated fat and no sugar in food preparation, and herbal medicines. He also promoted consumption of higher than typical amounts of nutritional supplements.

Rodale was well represented in the bookroom. I found *Sugar: The Curse of Civilization*, *The Healthy Hunzas*—about a tribe of people near the Himalayas sometimes called the healthiest people on earth—and a stack of *Prevention* magazines. I didn't read this material much. I mostly listened to my father and mother talk about it.

Rodale was the star of the long shelf of gardening books. There were *The Complete Book of Composting* and *The Encyclopedia of Organic Gardening*, among others. I learned that he was one of the pioneers of sustainable agriculture and organic farming in the United States. I didn't read much but instead was able to watch my father put it into practice in his garden.

There was another thing I discovered in the bookroom. In a rack on the desk were manila folders with handwritten papers. Prominent among them were sermon notes and prayers. I didn't venture into this territory often—just enough to get a childish feel for another part of the mystery. My dad valued preaching and teaching, and he prepared carefully. And he valued prayer—he wrote them out for use at church, which I imagine is why I had overheard church members express appreciation for his prayers.

To this day, I remember the smell of that room. Once in a while I catch a whiff of it—maybe in someone's home or a library—and it takes me back. I'm back in the room with all the black books and the gardening magazines and the sermon notes and handwritten prayers. The room still remains somewhat of a mystery, as does my father. But, as the stories that follow show, that room also became an unexpected launching place for a long journey, a journey that turned into a life project.

It's a journey that many of us embark upon in one way or another. We begin in a tightly circumscribed world. We don't even know at first that it is a circumscribed world. It is just our world, the way things are, and it feels like home. That small world is where the journey—if one decides to take it—always begins.

I

AWAKENINGS

CHAPTER 2

THE PAST HEAVY UPON US

> "The weight of our imperfect history lies heavy upon us."
> —Wilfred McClay

Since childhood I had been told that, in contrast to all "the denominations," Churches of Christ—my childhood church—originated straight out of the New Testament. It was the one true church, freed of all human tradition and fully restored according to the apostolic pattern after more than 1,500 years of desperate corruption, human creed-making, and rampant division.

It was a powerful vision. Heady in its logic. Convincing to many in its claims. In the nineteenth century, it created a burgeoning renewal movement of tens of thousands—eventually millions—of people.

I was raised on this vision. The air I breathed was thick with it from my earliest days. It seeped into my everyday consciousness. It formed my childhood view of the world I inhabited. For a good while it provided a strong sense of security, even of divine favor.

In my family this vision of the true church was deeply intertwined with other elements—a strong suspicion of "the world" around us, a strict dietary regimen, and a strong commitment to simplicity of life. By my early teens, questions had emerged and gnawed at me. I did not rebel—I was always the "good boy"—but there was a steadily rising urgency in me to figure out some things. I was pretty sure some answers lay back there somewhere, but I didn't know where to find them.

Finding them took a good long while. I didn't find anybody in my world able to guide me or even to really understand my questions. The questions had to do with what I would much later come to call the inescapable reality of tradition—the way tradition always shapes us in profound ways, whether we know it or not. I wanted to know what mine was and how it was forming my way of being Christian. In my early high school years I began to get a few glimpses of how this works. I remember reading Fawn Brodie's *No Man Knows My History* (1945), a critical telling of the Mormon founder's story, and Louis Cochran's *The Fool of God* (1958), a mostly uncritical telling of Alexander Campbell's story. I was fascinated. And some wheels began to turn.

My years at a Christian college were good and important years, but the things I sought were not readily at hand. A particular orthodoxy, rooted in this history, held sway, as one would expect, and answers to my questions were limited by those strictures. But this past rested heavy upon me. So strong were my questions—and so essential for me to figure out—that making the pursuit of them central to my future seemed inevitable. I had been a premed major, but medicine was not my future. Instead, upon graduation, I began nine years of seminary and doctoral work. It was the beginning of a life project.

Libraries and archives became a way of life during those seminary and doctoral years and beyond. Not because I loved the isolation or the feel of old books and papers, but because they were places to discover what I needed to find. There was the summer my family and I spent six weeks in Nashville, where each weekday I would drive to the Disciples of Christ Historical Society archives to immerse myself in the primary sources from the nineteenth century. Or the summer we lived in Chapel Hill, North Carolina, where I worked in three different archives. And there were other summers and shorter research trips.

Then there was Vienna. During a sabbatical semester my family and I lived in Vienna, Austria. Our three children were young—five, seven, and thirteen—and we backpacked around Europe before settling in Vienna. For eighteen weeks we got to explore that grand city, a city still marked by its former role as capital of the Austro-Hungarian Empire. We attended the famous Staatsoper and the symphony. We visited Mozart, Beethoven, and Strauss sites. Our five-year-old daughter attended an Austrian preschool and was speaking German with an Austrian accent by the time we left.

But my main occupation that semester in Vienna was reading Alexander Campbell's two journals, published from 1823 until shortly after his death in 1866. I read over ten thousand pages, writing hundreds of sheets of notes and wrestling mightily with the structure of his thought and the force of his personality. He was brilliant and voracious in his productivity, but (to me) irritating and off-putting in his manner. I was struck by his scornful dismissiveness and what someone has called his "rhetoric of ridicule." Through it all I came to like Mr. Campbell less and less. But I kept reading and taking notes week after week. The result was a deep well of knowledge that I would dip into often through the years.

It was a strange way to spend eighteen weeks in Vienna!

In a five-year period between 1988 and 1993, I authored or coauthored five books on the history and theology of Churches of Christ. All of them, to one degree or another, sought to answer the question, "Where did modern Churches of Christ come from—and why?"

A central focus was that the concept of "restoration" had a long history, that Churches of Christ and Barton Stone and Alexander Campbell didn't discover it. It went back centuries, where it had been a tool of Christian renewal in the face of particular challenges—"corruptions"—facing the church. The restoration impulse took different forms, depending on what the current deficiencies were judged to be. For Campbell the key defect was the proliferating divisions in the body of Christ in the free air of the United States. For earlier restorers—particularly the Anabaptists of the sixteenth century—it was nominal discipleship of Jesus in the context of a state church where "everyone" was Christian. Or it was the Puritans' passion for simple, unadorned worship in contrast to the elaborate liturgies, "inventions," and hierarchical structures of the Roman and English churches. Or it was the problem of a formal faith without much evidence of the Spirit's regeneration of the heart—as with John Wesley. The restoration tradition, it became clear, was long and strong—and it varied by time and place. It was a long Christian tradition furthered by those who tended to claim no tradition.

The challenge of those early books was to engage this long tradition. To acknowledge it, to learn about it, and then to critique it—but with respect and appreciation, similar to the way one might engage one's own family tree. It was a call to see how and why the tradition developed, to engage with its blemishes and blindnesses as well as its strengths and gifts. It was a call to place Churches of

Christ squarely in the stream of real human history, which was a new and jolting perspective for most members in the 1980s.

I had no idea how these new and critical perspectives would be received. The thought crossed my mind that I might lose my position at the Church of Christ-related university where I was employed. But to my great surprise, when the first books appeared in 1988, a door seemed to open. There was an amazing explosion of interest. Mail flooded in (it was before email). People throughout Churches of Christ, older and younger, seemed hungry for this fresh perspective.

The books, although measured and understated, represented an emotionally turbulent and spiritually unsettling journey for me. But a journey, it turned out, that spoke strongly to a multitude of people. Over the thirty-plus years since, I've realized what those books seemed to provide: a bridge. A bridge to a larger Christian mainland.

Other books followed, all of them seeking to provide orienting doors and windows into the past, and some seeking to help church members navigate the mainland. Over all these years, I've sometimes asked myself, "Why this life project? Why not medicine?" The answer to that question will emerge in the stories that follow.

CHAPTER 3

WINTER GARDEN

> "Childhood is the small town everyone came from."
>
> —Garrison Keillor

I came to boyhood in the Central Florida town of Winter Garden. It was surrounded on three sides by vast orange groves and on the other by Lake Apopka, which was twelve miles across. We lived on a dirt road a block from Main Street, which had an active train track running through the center of it and at one end an ice plant where they loaded box cars with giant blocks of ice.

One might be tempted to think that this little town—laid out among breaks in the orange groves all around—was idyllic and arcadian. It mostly seemed so for a kid who got to spend the summers roaming orange groves, catching bream and catfish around the edges of a lake that one could not see across, engaging in "wars" with the clusters of hard and sticky little dates from palm trees, and heaving swamp potatoes into the opposition's foxholes. I don't remember wearing shoes all summer except to church on Sundays and Wednesdays.

My sister graduated from high school the year I finished first grade, and then she was off to college. So I was in essence an only child. My bedroom became a workshop for various projects and hobbies—weather forecasting, musical instruments, gardening, magic, astronomy, to name a few. We had no radio or television in our house, so at around age seven or so I became a voracious reader, rejoicing each semester when the Scholastic Book Fair came around and my parents gave me money to buy a new stack. I loved *Big Red* and other books by Jim Kjelgaard, as well as the wide shelf of blue-backed biographies of famous athletes, race car drivers, scientists, politicians, authors, and others.

I would always get started on my latest hobby by bringing home a stack of volumes on the subject from the public library. One year—I think I was eleven—one of my book stacks focused on stories about advances in medicine made by famous physicians and medical researchers. Stories like Alexander Fleming's discovery of penicillin (1928), Robert Gross's first corrective heart surgery for infants (1938), and Jonas Salk and the polio vaccine (1953). Somehow during this time I decided—maybe it was after reading a *Boys' Life* article—that I wanted to be a brain surgeon when I grew up, an aspiration that would stay with me into my college years.

Three other memories from age eleven remain vivid: a girl named Ginger whom I met during a summer stay in Utah, my baptism in September, and John F. Kennedy's assassination on November 22. I recall sitting on our front porch in shock and grief, trying to comprehend the president's violent death. It haunted me for many days. A while later I learned that, on the very same day, C. S. Lewis—whose writings I was just discovering—had also died.

Summers in Winter Garden were a laid-back adventure. I would spend hours high up in our huge Japanese plum tree, amid the ripening of the plums. The plums were unique, and finding one at the perfect ripeness was an art. The birds were after them just as I was. Most plums had two or three seeds, but I learned to tell which ones had more—up to six or more. My all-time record was eight.

One summer I wore out two skateboards on the slalom course we set up on the sidewalks surrounding the Masonic Temple a stone's throw from our house. Another summer I joined a Cub Scout den that met at the old First United Methodist Church, and in the fall I became a card-carrying member of the 4-H club, where I entered my vegetables in the county fair and won a few ribbons.

Our lives were simple, and we had simple, well-established pathways: Lakeview High School where my father taught English, Dillard Elementary School where my mother taught fourth grade and where I attended, and church where we gathered three times a week.

For several years we had no automobile. Not because my parents couldn't afford a car, but because, in their judgment, we didn't need it. It was about a mile to church and about a mile to our elementary school and to the high school where my father taught. Occasionally, we would take a bus to shop in Orlando about fourteen miles away. And sometimes we would accept a ride home from church on a Wednesday night.

On Sunday evenings, on the walk home from church, I'd pass the small American Legion building a couple of blocks from our house and sometimes pause to watch through the windows as a small group of Pentecostal worshippers danced and sang with their electric guitars. That was about as exotic as it got for me in Winter Garden.

Jody Valdez, who lived around the corner on the next block, was one of my friends. His parents owned Modern Stationery on Main Street and were strong members of Calvary Baptist Church. Jody's cousin, Bert Valdez, who lived across town, was another friend. Bert and his parents, whom I would call "bohemian"—and definitely not church members—introduced me to new worlds: the world of orchids, bromeliads, and ferns; the world of rock collecting and gem polishing; the world of weekend craft fairs and art shows. It was with them that I ate for the very first time at a McDonald's restaurant. A hamburger was fifteen cents. It was 1962.

The only music I had access to at home was a set of twelve LPs introducing classical music. You could say I was culturally deprived when it came to rock 'n' roll and country music. But the great classical composers became my friends. In high school I did acquire a tiny transistor radio that I used to listen to rock 'n' roll with an earphone in bed at night—giving me a passable knowledge of sixties rock.

You could have a winter garden in Winter Garden. The temperature was often in the seventies and even eighties in December. We grew summer vegetables all through the "winter." Giant poinsettia bushes, which I have never seen outside anywhere else, were part of the landscaping around our house.

You could think that my town was idyllic. But there were telling signs that said otherwise. Our family doctor's office, I noticed, had a "colored" waiting room and a "colored" water fountain and a "colored" bathroom. At age seven I asked my mother about it, and she gave me a simple introduction to segregation. She told me about the separate schools. The Black part of town, mostly poor. Some of the embedded rules of separation. It was clear that she deplored it and sought in her own life to ignore and overstep the rules as much as she could. She said the teachings of Christ demanded resistance.

There were other signs that we were not in Eden. There was the death of my fifth-grade classmate, Gregory Gilley, who was hit by a car on his bicycle, and the suicide of the mother of one of my sixth-grade friends. And in the tenth grade there was the dark news of an eight-year-old girl in tiny nearby Ocoee who was abducted and murdered. Her name I still remember after all these years: Camellia Jo Hand. And many years later I learned that her killer was a young man born and raised in Siloam Springs, Arkansas, where I would later live for a decade.

And then in 1975, when I was in college, I heard the news about a quadruple murder at Zeigler's Furniture Store directly across the street from the church building where we had attended all those years. Tommy Zeigler, whom my father had taught in English class at the high school, was arrested and convicted. His wife, who had been a student teacher in my mother's fourth-grade class, was among the slain. You can never tell about small towns.

Someone has said that in our childhoods we develop a geography of the heart. I developed my geography in Winter Garden. For me, it is palm trees, orange groves, outdoor poinsettia bushes, huge oak trees draped with Spanish moss, and beautiful blue lakes. Wherever I see these things, it starts to feel like home.

CHAPTER 4

SISTER HAWTHORNE

> "What we remember from childhood
> we remember forever—permanent ghosts,
> stamped, inked, imprinted, eternally seen."
> —Cynthia Ozick

It is not possible to understand my childhood without understanding that our church was the center of our world. All that we did revolved around that most basic commitment. We of course always attended our church's three weekly gatherings—Sunday morning, Sunday evening, and Wednesday evening Bible classes. But it was far more than that. It was the fundamental way we ordered our world and focused on what mattered most in our lives.

I cannot remember a time when this was not true. As a small child I could not understand—and certainly could not articulate—the structure and elements of this conviction, except that it was about God, God's Son, and God's Word, the B-I-B-L-E. And that God had revealed a story, a plan, for people on earth. And that Jesus loved me. In the aura of that conviction, I sometimes sensed, even as a very young child, that there was a grand purpose for our lives and a special way of living that it entailed.

Many years later the Christian philosopher Charles Taylor gave me a way of naming what I experienced. He called it a "social imaginary." He described it as the way a group of ordinary people learn to imagine their social world even before they think much about it; it gets formed by stories, rituals, images, relationships, and particular beliefs. But it can't be adequately expressed as beliefs or doctrines because much more is at work—deep assumptions underlie it, and thick social practices play a key role in forming it. Everyone receives something like a social imaginary, mostly without even knowing it. It's what makes meaningful, long-term engagement in a group—or a culture—possible.

My earliest memories in church go back to about age four when we lived in Florence, Alabama. My father was the preacher for the Mars Hill Church of Christ a few miles outside the city. The building was a simple, white, classic wooden building with a small steeple. It was surrounded by pine trees and a few oaks. On Sundays, cars would be parked among the trees, and sometimes there would be a couple of horses and buggies tied up to trees. There were high rectangular windows inside but no ornamentation. And no air-conditioning. The hymnal racks contained cardboard fans—the kind with wooden handles and funeral home advertisements on one side and a sentimental picture on the other.

I remember the predictable rhythms of the worship services, the robust a cappella singing, the cadence of the sermons (which often seemed interminable), and the attentive reverence of the members. I would sometimes lie on the hard wooden pews, counting the ceiling tiles or, in summer, watching the ceiling fans revolve. I was taking it all in, although I couldn't tell you exactly what it was I was taking in.

When we moved to Winter Garden, Florida, our church seemed pretty much the same. Except it was in the city and constructed of cement blocks with asbestos tiles for siding. No ornamentation, except a wooden communion table with the words "This do in remembrance of me" engraved across the front. At the communion service every Sunday, the wooden service trays were covered by a white tablecloth, which the man presiding would remove at the beginning and replace at the end. I always watched in fascination when the trays were passed and members took the bread and the fruit of the vine. I was still taking it all in—by now I could name what they were doing and sort of why they were doing it. But I sensed that there was much more going on than I—or maybe anyone—could say.

Most all of us were in Bible classes every Sunday morning and Wednesday night. For several years my teacher was a woman named Inez Hawthorne. She was a somewhat reserved middle-aged woman with a firm yet pleasant manner. I remember the colorful lesson quarterlies we used, especially the Bible stories she told using a flannelgraph board. There were Jacob and Esau, Joseph and his brothers, Moses and Aaron, and all the rest—the whole host of Bible characters appearing as bright paper characters on the flannel board. And for a couple of years we received a weekly take-home "comic book" called *Sunday Pix* containing serial stories about a first-century young man—a Christian and a Roman—named Tullus. I was hooked.

We called her Sister Hawthorne. Her husband was not a church member, though he came with her every once in a while. I remember that her older son became a state trooper and that her younger son was the starting quarterback for the high school football team. She was a proud mother. And I remember that just a few years after I had moved out of her class and into the high school Bible class, the younger son, Don, was killed in an automobile accident. She continued to teach the younger children's Bible class after that.

Sister Hawthorne well represented the character—and the characters—of our church. Steadfast, committed, gracious, in many ways unremarkable. Showing up week after week, year after year, to teach the Bible stories to a bunch of sometimes unruly kids. An ordinary saint. Our modest congregation was full of them. Cecil Caldwell, a plumber, whose standard public prayer I could recite by heart; Tom Wise, a carpenter, and his wife, Geraldine, who were both probably wise but whom I mainly knew as warm and welcoming; Hugh Grimes and his wife, Doris, both realtors with a no-nonsense manner; Raleigh Brown, a fertilizer salesman, and his wife, Charlotte; Brother Janney, a rotund lifelong bachelor whose favorite Sundays were potluck dinner Sundays. And numerous others. Ordinary saints all of them. They called each other brother and sister—in Christ. And that's what they were, more or less.

Later, many years later, I would begin to put my boyhood church experience in the larger frame of the Christian tradition over the centuries, learning where it came from and its theological trajectory. But here it was simply my world, indeed *the* world, a world that was strong and stable and life-ordering. A world in which God was up to something—and we were a part of it. I was learning the story of God in Scripture, witnessing the lives of people who had followed Jesus seriously for many years, observing baptisms and newness of life, gathering weekly at the "Lord's table" where sisters and brothers shared in Christ's body and blood and were being trained (as the apostle John said) to "Love not the world, neither the things that are in the world" (1 John 2:15 KJV). Sister Hawthorne was a vital and unforgettable part of that world for me.

CHAPTER 5

FATHER'S TABLE

> "I believe that what we become depends upon what our fathers teach us at odd moments, when they aren't trying to teach us."
>
> —Umberto Eco

My father was forty-three when I was born. He had married my mother, Carolyn, in his early thirties, and my sister was born a year later. Then I arrived eleven years later, at a time in his life when my father seemed more ready to be a part-time grandfather than a full-time father of a little boy. My earliest memories are of a gray-haired man with rimless glasses, hair parted down the middle, who wore loose-fitting seersucker trousers held up by suspenders and white or tan long-sleeved shirts. He often wore sandals with white socks. Though he had a narrow face and slim build, his belly was full, making him look somewhat pear-shaped. One of my cousins later told me his face reminded her of Peter O'Toole.

My dad didn't fish, hunt, or attend sporting events. He didn't watch or follow football, basketball, baseball, or any other sport.

He didn't play golf, run, or bicycle. And he didn't have any friends, at least that I ever saw. He had brothers and sisters in Christ, people at church who admired him as a teacher and leader. But he had no "companions," to use C. S. Lewis's word, and certainly not any "friends" in Lewis's fuller sense of that word.

As far as I could tell, outside his job as a high school English teacher, he did five things: walk for his health, garden for his health, attend church and prepare lessons for church, read about healthy food, and prepare and eat healthy food.

If you asked me, I would say that his main thing was preparing healthy food. If you had asked him, he no doubt would have said his Christian commitment was the main thing. But you would have to understand that, to him, eating healthy food—stewardship of the body—was a central tenet of his understanding of Christianity.

To me, he seemed stern, distant, and mostly humorless. He spent most of his time outside of work taking care of himself—resting on the bed in his office, reading about nutrition and organic gardening, walking or digging in his garden for thirty minutes a day, and preparing food in the kitchen. He even skipped church most Wednesday evenings—said he wasn't up to it after a day's teaching—and I took that in stride, though I thought it out of character with his principles.

Beyond these activities, his life remained mostly a mystery to me. He did not play ball with me. He never fished with me. He did not read books to me. He did not take me on any adventures. He did not take me out to eat. He did not attend any of my sporting events—from Little League to high school track and basketball. He did not welcome my friends or participate in or initiate any of our activities. I do not recall a single party, celebration, or other social gathering in our home. Including Christmas, which he didn't believe in.

The one thing we did together was garden. "Together" would be putting it too strongly. Rather, I joined him in his garden, which was the one place a little boy could enter his world and learn alongside him. So I asked questions, watched his organic techniques, and listened eagerly to his disquisitions about the virtues of chicken manure, composting, and exotic greens like comfrey.

The dinner table provided a different kind of encounter with my dad. It was the place I was grilled and drilled on three topics of primary importance to him: healthy food, correct grammar, and true religion. I would listen to steady commentary, dish by dish, on the nature and merits of the food we were eating. And I knew my grammar would be screened for improper word usage, slippage in syntax, and mispronunciation.

"What did you learn in your English class today?" he would sometimes ask. And I would usually tell him something, if I could remember.

"We are learning to diagram a sentence," I might say. "So we are learning the parts of a sentence."

Invariably, he would ask a question. "What are the main parts of a sentence? Start with the subject—what's after that?"

If I was lucky enough to remember, I would say, "The predicate comes next, then the direct object, then the indirect object."

"Okay, that's good. Here's a hard one. What about a gerund? Do you know what a gerund is?" And I would say, "No, we haven't learned that yet."

Then he might answer his own question: "It's a verb that is made into a noun by adding *-ing*. So the verb *eat* becomes *eating*. *Eating* is a gerund."

I would continue eating, glad to know a little more grammar.

The other topic of dinner conversation was from the theology department, though he would never have called it that. (Theology was something we didn't do—we just read the Bible closely.) So he would occasionally instruct me on why our church was the one true church, why the denominations were all wrong, why we had "no creed but the Bible," and on the moral rules that governed our family. These rules included not only strict taboos against drinking all forms of alcohol, smoking (of course), watching television (which we never had), and gambling, but also the vice of extravagance or flashiness.

When I was in the eighth grade, I asked my parents if I could get a London Fog jacket, which was popular with the boys in my school. They were gray or black and one wore them with the collar turned up. They cost about twenty dollars—eight or ten dollars more than a regular jacket. My father said no. Too extravagant. Too fashionable. And unnecessary. My mother smiled wryly, knowing that would be the answer.

We were not Mennonite or Amish, but he preached against all forms of ostentation, which included bright-colored clothing, decorative home furnishings, and numerous other signs of what he viewed as worldliness. He would not allow my mother to wear bright-colored clothing, especially red. Tan was his color of choice, though light blue was acceptable if it was dull enough. He wore tan jackets and trousers, painted the walls tan, and slept under tan bedspreads.

Face cards were taboo in our house; they were used for gambling, and he wanted nothing to do with that. So my mother and I played Old Maid and Rook instead. I never saw my mother touch a deck of face cards all those years. But when my dad died in 1979—at age sixty-nine—a few weeks later she bought some cards and began playing canasta two, three, or more times a week. I know she missed him in certain ways in those years after his death. But she seemed mostly to relish her freedom.

In the decades since my father's death, I have wondered about his circumscribed world, his health fixation, his rigid commitment to a narrow set of rules, and his lack of joy. What were his fears? What drove him to such a boundaried existence? Why could he not receive a boy in need of a father's attention and blessing? And how did his strict and unbending practice of the faith relate to the theological questions that have driven my quest for a livable faith?

As I remember and wonder, I am reminded of the epigraph of this book: "Remembrance is necessary, but so, too, is forgiveness. We cannot live without both, and they cannot exist for long apart from each other."

CHAPTER 6

THE GOOD BOY

> "Once there was a boy who
> Never made his sister mad,
> Never whipped fer bein' bad, . . .
> Always fit fer folks to see,
> Always good as good could be."
>
> —Edgar Guest

I was always the model boy and the model teenager—the one that the mothers at church bragged about as the epitome of manners and maturity. I was kind, respectful of my parents and others, an excellent student, and conscientious in all my ways—and doubly so when it came to my desire to know and serve God.

My parents treated me mostly like a little adult, always assuming that I was reasonable, well-considered, seldom reactive, and able to occupy myself with constructive and creative activities. I was the kind of kid who was no fun for bullies; they couldn't hook me with their taunts and were mostly oblivious to me.

I was always the good boy. Never caused trouble at church, at school, at Cub Scouts, or anywhere else. No mischief. No bending or ignoring of the rules. Around other kids, I was always the first to heed a teacher's or supervisor's call for order and restraint. And I was usually the one who stood up for the kid being taunted or mistreated. That's how I got into my one and only fight.

Geraldine Wise, Charlotte Brown, Sister Summerford (in her eighties), Jo Swanner (the preacher's wife in her late twenties), and who knows how many other women at church would go on and on to my mother about how kind and considerate I was, how thoughtful and knowledgeable I was, what wonderful things I was going to do when I grew up. And how proud she must be of her son.

She was. And she would have these adult-like conversations with me about these admiring conversations. You would think all this might up the pressure for me to meet all these high opinions and expectations. Or swell my head. But it didn't. Because that was who I was. It didn't take much effort. I didn't much have it in me to cause irritation or create a ruckus or disrespect others, whether young or old.

Except when it came to a new kid at church named Randy Dungan. He was a teaser who could easily get mean; he didn't know when to back off. And he was a braggart who often tried to make himself look smarter and stronger and cooler than he was. He showed up one afternoon at the basketball court where my friend Jody Valdez and I were shooting baskets. He started teasing my friend, who was a bit awkward on the court. He began shoving him around, then elbowing him and making wisecracks. I asked him to stop. Then I insisted that he stop. Then I shoved him back when he kept on.

Suddenly, to my utter amazement, I lit into him with my fists, punching and grappling, then rolling in a clinch on the ground. I was a little bigger and stronger, and I soon overpowered him. It was over. I had never felt like this before. It felt really good. I later learned that I had just experienced an adrenaline rush.

That was my one and only fistfight. Nobody, as far as I could tell, ever knew about it, except Jody and Randy—and Randy wasn't telling. It turned out to be a strange anomaly, after which I continued to be the good boy.

The fight was not a topic of conversation at the dinner table that night. For one thing, I didn't know how to account for it—it was so out of character for me. For another, it was an element of a slowly growing part of my life that I mostly kept from my parents: the times I watched television at Jody's house without getting their approval for the shows, the unhealthy snacks and candy I sometimes accepted from friends, and my association occasionally with a boy named Ronnie whose outlook on life my parents wouldn't have approved.

The dinner conversation turned, as it often did, to the topic of healthy food. Sometimes it was initiated by my questions, but more often by my father's desire to educate me.

On the table was a bowl of baked sweet potatoes. We had been eating them more frequently in recent times. "How do you like sweet potatoes?" my father asked.

"They're good," I replied. "But I think they need lots of butter." My parents kept butter but used it very sparingly.

"Sweet potatoes are more nutritional than regular potatoes. That's why we are eating them more often." Then came the lesson: "They are rich in something called antioxidants and especially one antioxidant called beta-carotene. Antioxidants protect the body from substances that can cause inflammation and do various kinds of damage. And beta-carotene is an antioxidant that supports healthy eyesight as well as a strong immune system."

"Good to know," I said. I took a certain comfort in that, wondering if maybe these antioxidants might replenish something depleted in my fight. "But is it still good to eat regular potatoes? What benefit do they provide?"

"Yes, they're good. Especially if you eat the skin—a lot of their nutritional value is located right under the skin." I remembered a story he had told me a while back about a famine, maybe in Eastern Europe, where a child had survived—when his family died—because he had eaten discarded potato peels.

I think the conversation then moved to another item on the dinner table. Or maybe I asked why we never ate fried potatoes. Or fried anything.

Through it all I was the good boy—mostly. Which meant, in this case, that I strove with all my might to learn the healthy way, to understand what was good to eat and what was not. This way certainly didn't match up with my friends and their families. With them I faced steady dilemmas and temptations. Did I accept their offers of potato chips, Twinkies, Coca-Colas, hot dogs, french fries, homemade brownies, and packaged cookies? Well, yes, I did. And no, I didn't. Sometimes.

Halloween presented an unusual situation. My parents allowed me to go trick-or-treating with a couple of my friends. I was a ghost one year, a hobo another, probably a pirate the next. They made a deal with me: "Go for all the candy you can. But then sell it to us. You keep five pieces, and we will pay two cents per piece for the rest of it." So my friends and I raced all around the neighborhood for two hours filling our bags. I think I earned about three dollars for the evening.

I was generally glad to be a good boy. Its downside didn't really emerge until some years later. The habit of perfection—as we might call it—was an impossible standard, especially in the more fraught world of young adulthood. That reality would serve to make the plot of my life more complex.

CHAPTER 7

TIGER'S MILK

> "If you want to feel twice as good, take brewer's yeast."
>
> —Adelle Davis

My father was preoccupied—obsessed was more like it—with health and healthy food.

Healthy food meant natural, organically grown, and unrefined "living food" he called it. It meant organic seeds, nuts, and dried fruits ordered from Pennsylvania or California. It meant no sugar, no white flour, no pork, no candy, no shortening, no store-bought foods with preservatives, no hydrogenated oils, no fried foods, no coffee or tea, no colas. It meant shelves of natural vitamins (rose hips vitamin C, for example, not ascorbic acid) and supplements (brewer's yeast was a favorite), and strange concoctions of these things mixed with liquids ranging from homemade yogurt to garden greens ground up with pineapple juice. It meant grinding nuts and juicing a wide range of fruits and vegetables, which would appear in ever more exotic mixtures.

The centerpiece of his morning kitchen ritual—before he ground the organic nuts, poached the egg whites, and toasted his 100 percent whole wheat biscuit—was mixing up a thick, viscous concoction that may well be unique in the chronicles of the modern whole foods movement.

My parents called it Tiger's Milk. The name came from a boxed drink mix they saw at the health food store in Orlando, Florida, operated by Seventh-Day Adventists. (It was the late fifties, several decades before stores like Whole Foods Market became common.) The ingredients were prescribed by Adelle Davis, the nutrition guru, but the recipe was invented by my parents through long experimentation.

I don't remember—or never knew—all the ingredients, but the basic ones are unforgettable: brewer's yeast, soy lecithin, powdered kelp, homemade yogurt, mashed bananas, and whole milk. To the ordinary person who had the misfortune of tasting it, the drink was vile—literally undrinkable due to the gag reflex. My parents drank it with every meal and often as a between-meal snack. They took it in thermos bottles on short trips, and on long trips they packed the ingredients to make it. Through an astounding reorientation of their taste buds, they had learned to relish it, almost like most people would relish a handmade chocolate milkshake. To them it was an elixir of life.

My parents made me a slightly more palatable version by withholding one or two of the dark powders and adding a little honey. The key word here is "slightly." Nothing could mask or cut the powerfully bitter taste of the brewer's yeast. I would hold my nose and drain the glass in steady gulps. It took practice to suppress the gag reflex and keep from spewing it out of my mouth.

I drank Tiger's Milk from the time I was five or six until I left their house to go to college at age sixteen. It was the centerpiece and symbol of the Allen food regimen. No doubt it was one of the healthiest possible concoctions that a human body could ingest. No doubt it laid a strong foundation for my physical health as an adult. But Tiger's Milk was much more than that.

The story was that my dad had been a frail and sickly young man and that his discovery of natural foods had transformed his life. No doubt it was true. The experience seemed to have had all the force of a religious conversion. Right alongside the Bible were the writings of J. I. Rodale (*The Complete Book of Vitamins*, *How to Grow Vegetables and Fruits by the Organic Method*) and Adelle Davis (*Let's Eat Right to Keep Fit*, *Let's Get Well*). He made no bones about it: eating unhealthy food—defiling God's temple—was right up there with drinking beer, getting drunk, and smoking cigarettes.

The Tiger's Milk regimen represented a set of deep convictions —never fully articulated—about how life was to be lived in this world. One conviction was that eating healthy food was a key discipline in achieving a holy life. There was a right way to eat and a wrong way to eat, and following the right way was part of one's duty to God. Sadly, many people lived in ignorance of this way—just as many lived in ignorance of God's moral laws; they needed to learn the truth, change their harmful dietary habits, and embrace the healthy way, the way of life and vigor and holiness.

From a fairly young age, I had a hunch that this strict connection between healthy eating and Christian holiness was probably somewhat overdone. But it was hard for a kid to sort through it.

Another deep conviction was that mealtime was mostly a time for ingesting a carefully calibrated assortment of whole foods and supplements for the purpose of maintaining physical health—and holiness. Adelle Davis, who once said, "If you want to feel twice as good, take brewer's yeast," was the arbiter of food choice and menu selection. She insisted on organic and natural foods, no processed foods, fresh whole grain breads, and locally grown vegetables. My parents added a few extrapolations of their own. Meals were put together for the purpose of meeting the strictures of these elaborate requirements. Taste and preference were very secondary considerations. My mother, as a concession to me, occasionally made an apple pie using whole wheat flour, honey, cinnamon, and fresh apples—a welcome treat, and one of only two desserts I remember, except for fruit.

My parents did not consider themselves suffering deprivation under this Tiger's Milk regimen. To the contrary, they appeared to experience a kind of delight, even glee, over the wonderfully healthy food and supplements that made up all their meals and snacks. They seemed to have retrained their taste buds and appetites. And they seemed proud—even a little haughty at times—of the nutritional knowledge and skills they had acquired over the years.

This may explain their incredible discipline. My father held to his dietary strictures without exception wherever he went, which meant he either ate sparingly or took his food with him. At church potlucks he would eat lettuce salad (if it had no dressing), roast beef (if it wasn't too fatty), whole grain bread (if it happened to be there), and fresh fruit (if it had no sugar). In all my memory of living in his house, I recall no exceptions, no slips, no departure from the regimen. My mother was a little less fastidious, but not by much.

A little boy didn't quite know what to make of these almost religious culinary practices. Their spirit and fervor. The strict holiness code. The steady threats of defilement. I strove with all my might to learn the healthy doctrine and to eat by the code. For the early years I didn't have much choice, but it wasn't long until I was inducted into the clandestine joys of forbidden food: ice cream sandwiches, Oreo cookies, french fries, Zero bars, Cokes. My school friends—with their families' loose and unenlightened dietary habits—were the primary culprits.

It is probably not surprising for me to say that in the house of my childhood there were no "feasts," no festive gatherings of friends where food and drink became in some sense sacraments through which joy is shared and friendship forged. After all, who would want to attend a banquet where Tiger's Milk was the drink of choice?

Today, with only a little imagination, I can still taste the Tiger's Milk and feel its thick and lumpy texture in my throat. I worked for a long time to move out of the Tiger's Milk worldview. It was hard. I still eat pretty healthily, but no Tiger's Milk toasts for me. I have found that good wine with good friends is quite a bit healthier.

CHAPTER 8

THE COMFREY CURE

> "The Church now which has no creed but the Bible is, all things else being equal, the true Church of Christ."
>
> —John R. Howard (1848)

My father's garden, which I expanded in carefully planned ways, became a source of spending money for me. As my mother and father used the produce, they would estimate what it would cost at the supermarket and keep a tab; at the end of the week, they would add it up and pay me the amount. I thus became a small-time market gardener.

One of the more exotic greens in the garden was comfrey. It was an herb with large, rough leaves up to a foot long that grew in a thick clump. I suppose some people still grow it, but I've never seen it in any garden since my boyhood. My dad proclaimed that it had several wonderful qualities, including high levels of vitamin B12 and healing effects on the skin. He used it regularly.

Somehow a woman in town heard that we grew it and wanted to buy it from us. She lived alone, and I soon learned she was a devotee of something called Christian Science. I didn't know what that was; my parents told me it was a religion, based on the Bible, begun in the later nineteenth century. Alongside the Bible it was guided by the founder's volume, *Science and Health with Key to the Scriptures.* According to my parents, the founder wanted to "reinstate primitive Christianity and its lost dimension of healing." So healing prayer, a focus on natural foods, and a suspicion of modern medicine were key features.

Almost every week for a year or more I would pick a grocery bag of comfrey leaves from our garden and ride my bicycle to this woman's house. When I met her at the door she almost always had on a bathrobe and wore a furtive look. She would usually give me two dollars, which I thought was a good deal. The only downside was that I often had to listen to a discourse on the benefits of Christian Science. Sometimes she would even give me a newsletter to read. My parents said her religion sought to "restore" original Christianity, but that it was actually more like a cult than a Christian church. The only thing about her beliefs for which they had any sympathy was her passion for natural foods and herbal supplements.

My father prized comfrey as well. He would grind up the large, green, somewhat hairy leaves and combine the paste with pineapple juice, drinking it along with his beloved Tiger's Milk. And perhaps he used it as a poultice and ointment. Years later, I would learn that comfrey is a powerful herb and can have a serious downside. As a medical website put it much later: "Comfrey has toxic substances that can cause severe liver damage and even death. You should never take comfrey by mouth." Oh well, it didn't seem to hurt him or, as far as I knew, the Christian Science woman.

The comfrey cure turned out to be a kind of parable, I later thought, for the strict and pure nutritional aspirations of my father and mother. Strong benefits and blessings, yet some unforeseen downside that had a way of eventually showing up.

That year during the comfrey season, my father continued my education around the dinner table. The conversation often turned to church matters, sometimes initiated by my questions but more often by my father's desire to ground me.

"Do you know what a creed is?" he asked one evening. I didn't, or at least I wasn't sure. "A creed is a list of beliefs held by a particular denomination. It emphasizes the beliefs that make that church distinctive from other churches. The members are expected to embrace it."

"I don't think we in the Church of Christ have a creed, do we?" I asked. "At least no one has mentioned it."

"Yes," my father said, "we do have a creed, which might surprise you. But it is not a man-made creed like the creeds of the denominations. It is a divine creed. It's God's declaration of what we are to believe. It's the Bible and only the Bible."

I thought to myself, though I didn't say it out loud, "The Bible is a really big book, and it seems like a big challenge to summarize the basic things required for us to believe." I didn't feel at all competent to argue with him, so what I said was, "So what are the basic things that our church is expected to believe? And who determines what those are?"

"Well," he said, "one first has to be clear that the Bible is our only authority in religion. It's not human traditions. Not man-made creeds. Only the Bible. And then one has to learn to interpret it properly. One of the basics for proper interpretation is to call Bible things by Bible names, which means limiting our Christian vocabulary to the actual words in the Bible."

"Okay, so we stick to the words of the Bible. But how do we tell what the essential basics are?"

"Well, it takes some study, and a desire to find the truth. One meets God in the Bible, the Creator. And one meets Jesus, the Messiah, God's Son. That's the most basic. Then one reads in the New Testament, especially in Acts of the Apostles, about God's plan of salvation. And one can see clearly the nature and pattern of the church after it was established on the day of Pentecost."

I asked, "Has someone written down these most basic things so people who want to learn about being a Christian can easily find it?"

"Certainly," said my father. "We have booklets and lesson plans on how to become a Christian and on how to identify the Lord's church."

"I've seen some of these in the foyer of our church building," I said. "But these are not creeds, right? What makes creeds different?"

"No, they are not creeds. Creeds are usually official documents approved by a denomination. The problem is they create and maintain division. And they easily discourage ongoing study of the Bible. We want the Bible to be the only authority for our faith."

The conversation probably stirred more questions for me than it answered. I was just beginning to see a connection between my father's convictions and the books in his office. A day or two later, when he was still at school, I slipped into the bookroom and pulled off the shelf one of the volumes I was becoming familiar with: *Questions Answered* by Lipscomb and Sewell. I looked for their opinion of creeds. God will judge those "who add to or diminish from the word of God," Lipscomb wrote, "yet in every creed, every discipline, and every confession of faith in the land both these things are done."

In another volume, I found Alexander Campbell's view of creeds. He said he opposed creeds "because old parties were sustained by them, because they made new parties, and because they were roots of bitterness and apples of discord." Rejecting all creeds, he said, we take only "the apostolic writings as our *christian* creed, and use . . . only the exact words of inspiration."

I tucked this point away. It became clear to me that "no creed but the Bible" was a key conviction of my church. I would later wonder if it might have a downside—somewhat like the comfrey cure.

CHAPTER 9

ALL THE WAY IN

> "The pledge that we solemnly make in . . . our baptism into Christ is that we strive to reproduce his life before the world in our own lives."
>
> —David Lipscomb

In the entryway of our modest church building in Winter Garden was a tract rack containing numerous pamphlets about the Christian faith and the Church of Christ. It always contained a small pamphlet titled "Neither Catholic, Protestant, nor Jew." I had read it by the time I was ten, but by then its basic claim had already become a fixture in my identity. People commonly "classify the church of Christ," it said, "as just another denomination of the Protestant group. We would like to convey to them that the category does not fit." Though we "may possess some of the characteristics of Catholics, Protestants, and Jews," it insisted, "we are not members of any ecclesiastical group. We are just Christians only, members of Christ's church."

This claim was fundamental to how Churches of Christ understood themselves. I had learned this on many occasions around the dinner table with my parents as well as in my solitary forays into the bookroom. The conversation might go something like this:

"Dad, can I visit Jody's church with him? It's their Vacation Bible School!"

"Remind me what church that is," my dad responds.

"It's Calvary Baptist," I say.

"Yes, you may go once," he says, which surprises me. "But remember, it is a denominational church, not the Lord's church." The term "Lord's church," I had learned, was the usual way of distinguishing the Church of Christ from all the denominations.

"As you know, Son, the Lord's church is the one that was established on the Day of Pentecost described in Acts 2. The denominations arose much later, and have added to the apostles' doctrine. Many among them sincerely love God and seek to follow the Scriptures, but their churches have departed from the Word of God. We need to be careful not to join them in these departures."

Following this conversation, I would find an opportunity to sit on the floor in the bookroom and pull out a few of my father's books. The ones I was getting to know, like *Questions Answered*. Its view of denominations sounded a lot like my father. "There is no authority in the word of God for any denominations," said Lipscomb. "But the church of God, the body of Christ, is well-known and approved in the New Testament." He put it even more sharply: "All denominations are sinful; every one is formed by adding to the things God ordained." To form "a denomination is to form an institution of man over and above the churches or institutions of God."

I read further. One should not speak of "other denominations" since that implies that the Church of Christ is one. One should simply say "the denominations." So if any people "obey the gospel among denominations, the voice of God is, 'Come out from among them'; and this they must do, if they expect to be saved in heaven."

So I went to the Calvary Baptist Church VBS with my friend Jody. It was a lot like attending VBS at my church. Except they used a piano. I'm sure there were other differences, but I didn't see them that night. I had ventured into the world of the denominations.

Occupying my mind during this season was the question of baptism. I had known for a long time that baptism was meant to be a decisive marker in one's life. It was an immersion into Christ—into his death for our sins—and a rising into new life through his resurrection. It was a sign of forgiveness of sin through the death of Christ. And it was the point at which God added one to his church.

I remember talking one day at length with my mother about my baptism. And then later with my father. They didn't rush me. They said I should have a strong sense of my need for Christ, an awareness of wrongdoing, of sin. And I should be ready to follow and serve Christ, to have my life more and more patterned after his life.

They didn't articulate this—no one did—but I had the vague sense of being a kind of halfway member of our church. I had lived in the thick of the church all my life. I had learned the Bible well. I had been taught to imitate Jesus. And I loved Jesus (though that was not the primary language we used). Who was I in this church? I had not been baptized. I could not partake of the Lord's Supper. If I was not a Christian, what was I? I didn't even know how to ask the question, so I didn't really expect an answer.

I decided to be baptized a few months after I turned eleven. The language I had learned for this was "obeying the gospel." Much later I would learn the history of this term, which went back to the early nineteenth century, to a time when baptism had been somewhat displaced by a conversion "experience." The experience was to be minimized in favor of obeying God's command to be baptized. Thus obeying the gospel.

The practice of baptism was one of the key issues with "the denominations," as I discovered in the Lipscomb book. God ordained that to enter the kingdom, sinners "must believe the gospel, must repent of their sins, and must be baptized into Christ for the remission of sins." The denominations, in contrast, claim "that the sinner is pardoned, saved, before baptism and independent of it"; they thus make "void this command of God by their traditions."

My decision to "obey the gospel" focused on my growing desire to make Christ Lord, not on rejecting denominational teaching. My heart was tender and my desire to "put on" Christ utterly sincere. The days leading up to the baptism were full of excitement and a sense of momentousness. It took place on a Sunday night, when there was a smaller crowd, which helped me be a little less nervous.

I walked forward at the end of the sermon. The preacher knew I was coming. His name was Bill Swanner, a tall, thin young man of about twenty-eight, with thick dark hair and a prominent Adam's apple. He towered over me in the baptistry. He asked me to confess Jesus as Lord, which I gladly did. He then lifted his right arm into the air, saying, "I now baptize you in the name of the Father, the Son Jesus Christ, and the Holy Spirit for the remission of your sins."

No half member now. I was all the way in. It was one of the most wonderful times of my young life. The afterglow lasted for weeks, maybe months. Years later, I would find myself using Martin Luther's language, who in times of great temptation and spiritual depression would declare, "I have been baptized," thus claiming by faith the objective reality of his new life in Christ.

So it would be for me.

CHAPTER 10

WHAT MY MOTHER KNEW

> "Behind all your stories is always your mother's story, because hers is where yours begin."
> —Mitch Albom

My mother, Carolyn Odom Allen, was thirty-nine when I was born. She was fun-loving and had a zest for life. She enjoyed people, liked to tease, and had a strong reflex to "join up." She would have hosted parties and receptions in our house if my father had allowed it. Instead, what she did was play board games and card games with me: Monopoly (using dominos, no dice—the gambling thing again), Scrabble, Parcheesi, Rook, and Uno. She loved it. So did I.

She became an enabler of my hobby projects, helping me find, mix up, or buy the raw materials for creating things, ranging from paper-mache and tempera paints to poster board and balsa wood. And she was the one who would smile with delight and approval at my handiwork, often encouraging me toward the next level or stage of my creations.

Mom taught fourth grade at Dillard Elementary School, walking the mile to school and back each day. During my three years at her school, I would usually walk with her. She had a television in her classroom, and I looked forward to watching it for half an hour after school some afternoons.

Like my father, Mom was obsessed with nutrition and healthy food, but with somewhat looser edges. Once in a great while, she made pan-fried potatoes and banana pudding (with honey, of course). She was probably more knowledgeable about the world of natural foods and vitamins than my father. She loved Tiger's Milk just as much.

Like my father, my mother was an ardent Christian, which meant she read and studied the Bible intently, sought diligently to reflect the fruit of the Spirit, and gave generously to others. And for her, following Jesus meant she did not cut her hair (in support of which she cited 1 Corinthians 11:15). She wore her hair in a bun and wore a hat to every church service—again as a matter of scriptural conviction (1 Cor. 11:4–6). She was almost always the only woman wearing a hat. She didn't make a big deal of it; in fact, she hardly ever talked about it. She just wore it.

In church, whenever a prayer was led—I will never forget this—she and my father would slip off the wooden pew and touch at least one knee to the hard floor. I asked her about it once when I was probably seven or eight, and she simply said, "It shows reverence to God and is one of the proper postures for prayer." That's all she said, and I didn't ask again.

Mom developed arthritis in her right hand in her late forties, so things like ironing became harder for her. This was back in the days when clothes were not wrinkle-free and had to be steam-ironed. For a few years she hired a Black woman named Bertha to iron for her on Saturdays. My mother would often sit with Bertha and talk—about family, about the Bible, about their lives.

Bertha was a Baptist, and my mother wasn't sure that she was a real Christian. Sometimes Mom would read the Bible aloud to Bertha, along with articles from Church of Christ magazines, hoping Bertha might come to know the way of the Lord more perfectly. Bertha seemed to love the Scripture reading, and the two of them developed a good friendship.

Bertha had a high-school-aged son named David. He was interested in college but didn't have the money or the knowledge of where he might be able to attend. It was 1962. My mother told Bertha about Southwestern Christian College, a predominantly African American school in Terrell, Texas, affiliated with Churches of Christ. David was interested and pursued it. My mother offered to pay much of the tuition. To all of their delight, David was accepted to Southwestern, and the following August, he left Winter Garden to begin college in Texas.

David thrived in college, both as a student and as a Christian. He was baptized and became a member of the Church of Christ. When he came home at the end of the school year, he called my father on a Saturday afternoon to ask if he could come with us to the Church of Christ, since there was no African American Church of Christ in the area. My father said, "Of course. You are most welcome to join us."

David met us at the church building on Sunday morning, and together the four of us entered the sanctuary and walked about halfway down the aisle to our usual seating area. A few people greeted us. After we were seated, I saw on the other side three families rise and begin to make their way out. They did not return. After the service my parents told me the three families left in protest of David's presence.

I was shocked. At the Sunday dinner table, my mother and father spoke their minds. "Son, we are deeply disappointed at what happened this morning," my mother said. "We had hoped that our congregation might have grown to the point it could welcome Black people into our midst. But we feared this might happen."

Before I could say anything, she continued, "I think you know our strong conviction—that this kind of prejudice is wrong. It is sinful. God is no respecter of persons, and Christ died for all of us. We stand on equal ground. All Christians are our brothers and sisters." She was almost in tears, but there was a strong and firm edge in her voice.

My father spoke up: "We will face this matter as a church. We must! The three families that left are core families, but I don't think they will return unless we give assurance that this won't happen again. And we will do no such thing."

My parents' response was not a surprise to me. They had been open over the years about their convictions. And I had seen them stand for their convictions without hesitation or embarrassment.

This event at my church happened in 1963, a time when the civil rights movement was in full swing and on the eve of the passage of the Civil Rights Act of 1964. The historical record shows that, in the midst of this momentous time, White Churches of Christ were almost completely silent on the subject of race and sought mostly to maintain the segregationist status quo. Carl Spain of Abilene Christian College delivered in 1960 a prophetic call to repent and to desegregate the all-White Christian colleges. And in 1961 *The Christian Chronicle* newspaper began publishing a few editorials inviting a dialogue on race. But for the most part, the issue of race was not viewed as a problem. "We do not believe that segregation has ever been a problem for the Lord's church," wrote a prominent

White editor in 1964. "The kingdom of heaven is the most completely integrated institution we know, and all the brethren accept all the brethren as brethren."

My mother didn't believe it. Not for a moment. She knew too much Bible for that.

My mother was a person who believed what she said and lived it. She was a profoundly *good* influence in my life.

CHAPTER 11

SEASONS OF HOOPLA

> "Souls are like athletes that need opponents worthy of them if they are to be extended and pushed to the full use of their powers."
>
> —Thomas Merton

In 1969, as a sixteen-year-old senior in high school, I was selected—to my great surprise—as an all-conference basketball player in our ten-team Central Florida athletic conference. I had been on the varsity team for two years at my small Christian high school in Mount Dora, Florida. Between my junior and senior years, I had grown two inches—to 6'3"—and added forty pounds, a circumstance that helps explain why I became a starter. I also had an accurate twenty-foot jump shot.

For some years our team had been very competitive in the conference, even though several schools were considerably larger than ours. These included Mount Dora High School, Tavares High School, Montverde Academy, and Howie-in-the-Hills Preparatory

School, among others. We even made an annual trip up to Valdosta, Georgia, to play Georgia Christian School.

We were a run-and-gun, high scoring team. I think we averaged around ninety points a game (with eight-minute quarters). A key reason was our 5'8" point guard named Monty Boyd, who was quick as lightning with a strange-looking but deadly shot from the top of the key. He averaged over thirty-five points a game. Coach Cletus Stutzman drove us hard. To get in shape for the season, the whole team was required to work out with the cross-country team—and three of us actually made the seven-member team. The conditioning paid off. We were conference champions my senior year, and three of us—Monty; Bob Hickman, our 6'1" center; and I, a shooting forward—were selected as all-stars.

It was a strange and unexpected capstone to my modest athletic career.

I would say that it began in elementary school in my mother's fourth-grade classroom. She had a television in the room and she would invite me—mostly on weekends but sometimes after school—to her classroom to watch it. To watch sports, that is, especially the Boston Celtics—with John Havlicek, Bill Russell, and Sam Jones—against whomever they were playing. Or Major League Baseball. Or sometimes college and NFL football. Like my father, she really didn't think television was good for much, but unlike him, she thought sports were good for a boy.

At about the same time I tried out for Little League baseball. I made it, and I ended up playing—mostly second-string—for the Cubs. Just wearing the green jersey and cap made me feel like I had a new status in the neighborhood. A couple of years later, it was time, I decided, for basketball. There was no team or tryout in sight, but it was time to learn to shoot baskets. My mother helped me buy a basketball, and on a nearby asphalt tennis court—which had a goal with a chain net on one side—I began practicing. Almost every day. After about six months, I had a good two-handed set shot, and I could make eight out of ten free throws.

I continued occasionally to watch basketball on television, where I observed more closely the players' techniques. I saw that the two-handed set shot was "old school" and that the one-handed jump shot was the big weapon. So I changed. It was awkward at first, but after a few months of daily practice, I was back to 80 percent free throws. And with more months of practice, the shot became a scoring weapon in pickup games. After more than two years of almost daily practice—mostly alone but once in a while with a one-on-one or two-on-two game—I set my sights on trying out for the junior varsity team. And so began my modest, three-year basketball career.

Since my school was twenty-five miles away and I was thirteen years old, my mother always had to pick me up from basketball practice and from games. Most days it was an hour and a half roundtrip for her. I don't think she missed any home games those years. She did not complain; indeed, she was an unrelenting fan.

Before and after the basketball season I ran cross-country and track—one in the fall and the other in spring. For two years I was usually in the fifth position on the seven-man cross-country team. We had one star who almost always finished at or near the front of the pack, and several others of us were strong to pretty good runners. One year we went to the state championship meet in Gainesville, where I think we finished in the top fifteen. But the main goal for me was to be in shape for basketball.

In three spring track and field seasons, I ran what used to be called the 880 (now the 800 meters). My friend Steve Christlieb, whom everyone called Tonto, wasn't built like a middle distance runner, but he ran a very good high school mile. I ran only a moderately good half mile, even though I did win a few races. The most memorable—and painful—part of track was the training sessions, where we usually ran eight quarter-mile sprints with only a short rest in between.

But basketball was the centerpiece. Our school had a basketball tradition. A few years earlier the team had been state runner-up, and most years we had won the conference championship. The coach brought an intensity to practices and to the bench at games. He broke more than a few clipboards expressing his displeasure. At home games our gymnasium was filled to capacity and pitched to a high decibel level. Home games were broadcast on the radio. The players were treated to a hero's welcome by the crowds. There was definitely a lot of hoopla.

My father attended a total of one game during those three basketball seasons. And at that one game—so someone sitting near him later told me—he went walking outside during much of it. He never saw me run track.

I played a lot of basketball in the years that followed high school. Intramurals with my college social club. Intense pickup games during my doctoral work at the University of Iowa. And in the NBA for over ten years—the Noon Basketball Association—at the university where I taught for fifteen years. Over one memorable semester, another professor and I, along with one of our graduate students, took on a couple of young local ministers and another grad student in a series of maybe fifteen three-on-three games. We never lost a game. Over the years since, it's been fun to rub it in.

The Boston Celtics have remained a favored team. But track and field has been the sport I've followed. I ran the half mile, my daughter ran hurdles in high school, and my younger son ran cross-country. For five years, I served as a track and field official for the Arkansas Razorback Track Club, where I worked many Southeastern Conference meets. And to this day, my son Daniel and I still attend as many major track meets together as we can, though he lives eight hundred miles away.

I look back on my three-year athletic career as the vehicle of a deep life lesson. The intense basketball workouts, with Coach Stutzman yelling in our ears, and the grueling training regimen for track and cross-country, with its not uncommon gut-wrenching aftermath, taught me something deep and true: we need to be pushed, trained, to the full use of our powers. For me, the lifelong fruit was a spirit of determination and perseverance. It may have been that spirit that would carry me through the long desert season that was to come.

II

CALLINGS

CHAPTER 12

RHETORIC AND ROMANCE

> "Deeper than the deepest ocean
> is the depth of my devotion,
> And so I bring all my love to you."

I ended up at Harding College in the summer of 1969 by an odd set of circumstances. I had already been accepted by another Christian college and was offered a good scholarship; I was planning to begin there in August. In early June, I set out with my parents on a cross-country car trip from our home in Florida to Portland, Oregon, where my sister and her family lived. We had decided to pass through Searcy, Arkansas, home of Harding, since both parents had attended there and wanted me to see the campus.

At our motel just outside Searcy, my parents got into a serious and prolonged argument on Friday night. There had been a pattern of that over the years, and it almost always threw me into an emotional tailspin. To escape it, I fled the motel and began hiking along the two-lane highway, going nowhere. I was distraught. My only thought was to get away. Returning to the room over an hour later, I announced that I would terminate my trip right there and enroll at Harding for the summer session, which was beginning on Monday. My parents conceded, and I did just that, thus beginning my college career two months early. I was sixteen years old.

Settling into college life was mostly a relief. The summer roommate, the cafeteria meals, the small summer classes, a few new friends—all of this I took in stride. Except for one thing: a male graduate student in education warmly befriended me and then after a few weeks made sexual advances to me. I was very naïve, and it left me confused and angry. Not knowing what to do, I immediately distanced myself, but I didn't tell anyone, and I quietly tucked it away as a college learning experience.

My courses over those early years—looking back after many years of academic work—were mostly unexceptional. Except for two. Which is to say that two courses in particular awakened something in me—loosed something in me—that proved revelatory. One was a course with the unexciting title of Composition, Rhetoric, and Research. I took it during the second semester of my freshman year. It was an honors class that met on the third floor of one of the oldest classroom buildings—in a sleepy, classic-looking room with no particular charm. Twenty students and a young professor named Nancy Banowsky Myers. The main textbook was *Language in Thought and Action* by S. I. Hayakawa (who became a US senator in the later years of his life). It was a widely used book on semantics focusing on the function of language as a symbol system and its vital role in forming a cohesive people able to govern themselves and to prosper.

I don't remember a lot from the book, though maybe its ideas became so embedded in me that I cannot remember their acquisition. What I do remember is the writing. We were assigned a series of essays that were to be shared in class. I spent hours on each one, and I found myself both challenged and delighted in ways I had not experienced before. I would call it enthralled. Enthralled by words and their possibilities.

The other course was English Literature, taught by Dr. Jo Cleveland, who was already something of a legend at the college. We read selections from Alexander Pope, Jonathan Swift, Emily Brontë, Lord Byron, William Wordsworth, Samuel Coleridge, and others. With enthusiasm and just the right touch of background and color, she made it possible for some of us to fall in love with the stories, poems, and essays of the eighteenth and nineteenth centuries.

I was still a premed major. But by my junior year, that got eclipsed by the humanities and writing and by the biblical and historical questions that had been brewing in me since my preteens.

But the premed chemistry labs had been good for something, it turned out. One semester, a blonde girl who sat at a table near me walked over and asked me a question about the lab assignment. I told her the steps I had taken in the assigned experiment, and my advice seemed helpful. She asked another time or two. Good chemistry, I guess.

The next semester, a good friend of mine and fellow member of my social club asked the same girl—her name was Holly—to be his date on our daylong club outing. He had no car. And I had no date. I drove, with Holly sitting between us in the front seat. She later said that by the end of the trip, she was much more interested in the driver than in her date.

Before long I asked her out, and we began dating. I was eighteen and had never had a girlfriend before. In high school I had gone to my junior–senior banquet with a girl from my church, but that was it. For me this relationship was something entirely new. Somehow I learned that she was also dating a handsome, blonde-haired, somewhat older student named David. So I pressed my case, and the next thing I knew, David was no longer a rival.

We corresponded all summer while she was on a choral trip in Europe. In the fall semester we ate meals together in the cafeteria. We studied together in the evenings. We went to church together. We sat in the campus swings together for long conversations. Her upbringing in Churches of Christ was almost precisely like mine. Her parents were devout members—her father a longtime elder like mine. And like me, she had always been a dutiful and respectful "good" child.

One big difference between her family and mine was Christmas. That first Christmas at her house was thrilling: lights in the front yard and on top of the house; a big tree with garish ornaments; wreaths, angels, tinsel, and Christmas stuff I'd never seen before; a feast for Christmas dinner, with homemade fudge sauce and ice cream in the evening. And of course, a mound of wrapped presents, including some for me. I was like a child.

That was the Christmas I asked her to marry me. We were nineteen. Our parents thought we were too young, which we were, but they both ended up giving their blessings, depending on our lifelong Christian training to see us through. A few weeks before the wedding, my mother wrote: "Son, I believe you have every good chance to rise above the many mistakes Dad and I have made over the years. . . . Always try to love Holly through thick and thin; for the 'thin' will come."

The wedding was set for early April in her hometown. We took a day off from classes, drove the sixty miles to her hometown, and got married. It was a medium-sized church wedding, with bridesmaids and groomsmen and a small chorus of singers. But something totally surprising happened when the bride entered the sanctuary. At the moment she started down the aisle on her father's arm, she looked straight at me and began singing a song.

> I come to offer my love to you,
> yours to have and cherish your whole life through.
> Deeper than the deepest ocean
> is the depth of my devotion,
> And so I bring all my love to you.
> In sorrow, in sadness,
> in joy or care,
> You need never fear tomorrow,
> for I'll always be there.

There were two other verses, and she sang the whole song while walking slowly down the aisle of the sanctuary. With her father beside her. She had told no one, not even her father. I was astonished and barely held it together.

The ceremony was conducted by our two fathers, my father addressing me, Holly's father speaking to her. My father—looking straight at me—said that marriage was "God's arrangement from the beginning; but when Christ came he gave the relation a new dimension, and I hope you will tremble at this obligation, for you are to be the same kind of head Christ is to his church." He said that "from now until the end of your lives, Holly is the most important person in the world to you." (I know he said exactly these words because, after his death, I found the handwritten manuscript of his remarks.)

Holly's father also exhorted her to faithfulness and lifelong commitment, with a generous sprinkling of Scriptures. After saying our vows, which we each had written, and receiving the pronouncement, we kissed and flew down the aisle together. Then off on a weekend honeymoon, and back to school on Monday.

"You need never fear tomorrow," she sang, "for I'll always be there." And she has.

CHAPTER 13

SIMPLE ENGLISH

> "The truth is that Simple English is no one's mother tongue. It has to be worked for."
>
> —Jacques Barzun

In the fall of 1972 I was newly married and in my senior year of college. The previous school year I had given up my premed major and decided on a Bible major (with a double major in general science). I had begun preaching each Sunday at a congregation in tiny Cherry Valley, Arkansas. It was a new experience, not terrifying but certainly daunting. Sunday sermon time rolled around with alarming frequency. And though I had heard many hundreds of sermons by that time in my life, I had no settled sense of how I should go about it. So I scoured the resources at hand for guidance and examples, and I began a process of homiletical experimentation. To the small congregation, my offerings seemed acceptable, sometimes even appreciated.

In our modest little apartment, I set up my own bookroom, consisting of a few shelves of books I had accumulated from courses and from recommendations I had picked up from various sources. A few titles came from my father. I began to imagine what a personal theological library should look like. And I began something else—this was long before personal computers: a topical filing system with manila folders, along with a 3" x 5" card file for alphabetizing book and article references. In creating these files, I had weekly sermon writing in mind, to be sure. But I also had a much larger horizon in view.

Right then and there I began envisioning the writing that I felt sure would accompany my continuing quest for answers to the big questions I had been asking for nearly a decade. I was on my way, but just barely. I didn't know where it would take me or what the results might be. But the resolve took shape during that year; it hardened and became a bedrock of my emerging sense of vocation. And it never went away.

In the few years that followed, I read a lot, usually with an eye to the writing itself. What was going on with the words and sentences? What made them strong, engaging, even moving? What made them clear? What made the writing sing? And I read *about* writing: Jacques Barzun, William Zinsser, Donald Hall, other standard works of the time. I tried to take to heart advice about the craftmanship of writing. Like Jacques Barzun's comment: "The truth is that Simple English is no one's mother tongue. It has to be worked for."

I set out to work for it.

I entered seminary the year after graduation, and there—among courses in biblical exegesis, theological research, church history, and theology—I proposed an independent study on writing to one of my professors. For this course, I pulled together and synthesized what I took to be the basics of the writing craft. The final project was a thirty-page paper on the nature and challenges of writing as a Christian calling. Here are a couple of excerpts:

> Rewriting is the essence of writing. We must convince ourselves that we are working in clay, not marble, that we are working on paper, not carving eternal words in granite. Only then will we understand that in a first draft we are merely creating a substance to be carefully molded in successive drafts.
>
> The word craftsman pays attention to the cadences and sonorities that distinguish moving prose from merely informative prose. Readers read with their ears as well as their eyes. They listen for the sound of words. The good prose writer doesn't let his sentences move along at the same plodding gait that will lull a reader to sleep. Instead, he uses variety: he reverses the order of a sentence, alters the length from short to long or vice versa, or substitutes a fresh word for one that is overworked. The writer strives for what we could call a poetic touch, which is an ephemeral quality of good writing that persuades and attracts but that cannot be explained by correct grammar or impeccable logic. It is a mystery appreciated and studied by writers dedicated to their craft.

Such pronouncements were a bit audacious for a twenty-two-year-old. But I was working for it. I wanted "Simple English" to become my mother tongue.

A well-known writer was once asked by a college student, "Do you think I could be a writer?" The writer replied, "Well, I don't know. But here's one good indicator: Do you like sentences?" I realized that I liked sentences. And paragraphs. And collections of them. The whole bit.

It would be fourteen years before the first books were published. Over this time there were many research papers, essays, journal articles, book reviews, and sermons. And one very long dissertation. After all this, writing was still not easy, certainly not automatic, but it was becoming a way of life, a central part of my vocation.

One thing I found myself often doing over the years was reading what I had written out loud. Sometimes it was to Holly—occasionally to someone else who would listen. No one had said I should do that—it was just my natural impulse, and I found it helpful in the revising process. So it was with a wry smile that I recently read this advice from a writer whom I admire: "Always read what you have written aloud. . . . This is not to say one must imitate natural speech; it is only to say that one must try to capture its rhythms. If what you have written is awkward on your tongue, then it is awkward on the page."

And this reminder from the same writer: "With words, we create worlds—in imagination, in the realm of ideas, in the arena of history. With words, we disclose things otherwise hidden, including even our inward selves." In writing, he says we "attempt to weave a spell." I like to think that I have woven a few spells over the years. But I can say, at least, that my writing has been better for knowing that weaving a spell was always possible.

CHAPTER 14

DEATH ONE SUNNY AFTERNOON

> "And what of regrets? . . . I shall allow them to . . . intensify the hope for that Great Day coming when we can all throw ourselves into each other's arms and say, 'I'm sorry.'"
>
> —Nicholas Wolterstorff

After I completed a master's degree in biblical studies and a year of additional work in theological studies, Holly, David (ten months old), and I moved to Iowa, where I had a fellowship at the University of Iowa School of Religion. As these years of study stretched out—three years of master's work already completed and six of doctoral work—my wife's parents would sometimes ask her (but not in my presence), "When is your husband going to get a job that pays money?" And she would say, "When he's far enough along with his degree."

The doctoral program was long and rigorous—some thought unreasonably so. For the first couple of years, students had to "qualify" in three broad areas: mine were Scripture, church history, and theology and ethics. Then for the next couple of years—after demonstrating reading ability in two modern languages—each student specialized: my specialization was the history of Christian theology in modern Europe and North America. I took focused seminars on Martin Luther, John Calvin, Puritanism, the Enlightenment, Søren Kierkegaard, nineteenth-century theology in North America, and a few others. Finally came the dissertation, which took another couple of years—and more.

A central part of my program was learning to interpret Christian movements in the context of their times. These contexts ranged from the late medieval world of Martin Luther, with its "introspective conscience," to the early nineteenth-century world of Barton Stone and the frontier revivals, down to the late nineteenth-century Progressive Era in which the Fundamentalist Movement emerged.

Here's one example of what this looked like. George Marsden's groundbreaking book, *Fundamentalism and American Culture*, was published in 1980, and I spent two weeks that year poring over it, fascinated by the complex story it told. The author laid out a rich picture of the sweeping intellectual and social changes that occurred after the Civil War and how that new environment challenged the reigning Christian orthodoxy. A loose federation of alarmed Christian leaders emerged seeking to resist efforts to bring the faith into line with the new progressive thought. These new cultural forces thus helped call forth a new type of conservative Christianity. It was called Fundamentalism—after a series of small volumes titled *The Fundamentals* (1910–15). Churches of Christ stood mostly outside this Fundamentalist coalition, but there were unmistakable similarities that struck close to home.

Along with my studies, I served as a teaching assistant in the most popular course on campus: Quest for Human Destiny, which enrolled about five hundred students each semester. The lecturer, a Reformed Jewish rabbi, was mesmerizing. One day a week the students were divided into classes of twenty-five, and I was one of a team of PhD students who conducted those classes, including testing and grading.

My main advisor and dissertation director was professor Dwight Bozeman, noted for his book *Protestants in an Age of Science: The Baconian Ideal and Antebellum American Religious Thought* (1977) and for his book on American Puritanism, *To Live Ancient Lives: The Primitivist Dimension in Puritanism* (1988). He was writing *Ancient Lives* during the years I worked with him, and his work shaped my dissertation research on Roger Williams, the founder of Rhode Island. Williams was a radical Puritan who became a Baptist for a short time and then a de-churched Seeker. An early fruit of this years-long research was an article titled "The Way to Lost Zion: Roger Williams and the Restoration of the Primitive Church."

My father knew none of this. Strangely, he never asked what I was studying in graduate school or what I thought about what I was discovering. He seemed to not want to know. His steady concern was that my studies—since they involved the world of theology—would shipwreck my faith. So at least once a year he would send me a long, handwritten letter—what could be called a jeremiad—warning me about the quicksand of "theology," its threats to the "Lord's church," and other associated pitfalls.

One of those letters said: "I continue to be concerned about you throughout these years of graduate study. It's very easy to be led astray by what the apostle Paul called 'vain philosophy' and the traditions of men. Stay close to the Bible and to sound teaching. Be ever on the alert and 'continue constant in prayer.'" In another letter, he wrote, "It is of the utmost importance that you stand fast in the teachings of true Christianity and not let yourself get led into a denominational view of the church. The Lord has one church and I hope and pray that you remain loyal to it." Once in a postscript he couldn't resist adding, "Do you need kelp tablets? We have quite a few."

During these doctoral years in Iowa, our son David was a preschooler. An eager, intense, and precocious preschooler. I was engrossed in my studies and absent too much—and when present, too often distracted and impatient, I'm sorry to say. But we still did things together. At about age two he got his first Lego set and, over the years that followed, became a Lego master, engaged for hours at a time. Sometimes I would join him on the floor for thirty minutes or an hour. One year we put together a Styrofoam sailplane with a six-foot wingspan and flew it together occasionally. And one spring we found a wounded baby bird in our front yard, which we—mainly David—fed and nursed back to health, and we got to see it fly away one day. For two summers we had a verdant and productive garden in our backyard. David enjoyed the intrigue of growing vegetables, and he especially loved picking (and eating) sugar snap peas in the spring and digging potatoes in the late summer.

Besides being intense and precocious, I would also call David straightforward and . . . bold. One time we were waiting for the city bus when a man walked into the glassed-in shelter while smoking a cigarette. David promptly informed the young man: "You shouldn't be smoking. It will cause cancer." Another time we were in the grocery checkout line behind a woman, and David, age four, spotted a box of Frosted Flakes in her cart. He walked over to her and said matter-of-factly, "Those sugary cereals aren't good for you; they can make you fat and give you diabetes." I think my parents had made a recruit!

David's boundless energy (one year he built a family of twenty-one snow-people), frequent questions ("Why do you have hairs in your nose?"), fix-it mentality ("I know what's wrong with the heater; the pilot light is out!" [he himself had blown it out]), floppy blonde hair (from his mom), and light blue eyes (from both his grandfathers) imbued our years in Iowa with a lightness, a brightness that healthily countered the numbingly cold winters and the intensely depleting doctoral studies.

My parents lived in Oregon during these years, and we typically visited them at least once a year. My father had begun experiencing mild to moderate dementia, probably Alzheimer's. My mother said he spent a lot of time trying to learn a couple of sermons so he could preach them again. He would walk around the house carrying the handwritten notes, and he would sit on the porch with them, reading and rereading—but mostly distracted. And then one day she called to say he was in the hospital with pneumonia and that his condition was worsening rapidly. The airlines were on strike, and we were unable to get there. He died three days later. He was sixty-nine years old; I was twenty-seven.

The memorial service and burial were held in the little town of Russellville, Alabama, his birthplace. My mother and sister, both living in Portland, Oregon, were present, along with Holly and David (then age three), plus a number of cousins, nieces, and nephews. My mother had requested the night before that I say some words.

The day of the service was sunny and cool—a very fine Alabama afternoon. About sixty people gathered in the chapel of the funeral home. The casket was open. He was dressed, of course, in one of his light tan suits. The minister from the Russellville Church of Christ delivered a eulogy and a short sermon. When it was my time to speak, I stepped up to the podium, paused, then began.

> I would like to share with you three things that make up what I consider my father's legacy to me. First, some of you know that my father was a devotee of healthy food—natural, organic, unrefined, unprocessed, unadulterated, even sometimes unpalatable—like a drink he called Tiger's Milk. I would wager that most of you here today would not be able to get this drink down. But seriously, this is a gift he gave me—a healthy foundation for my life.

My voice was perfectly calm.

> Another legacy he left me was his care with words. He was an English teacher. Grammar mattered to him. A strong vocabulary mattered. Good expression mattered. From an early age I learned to care about the sound of words, the play of language. Sometimes it was irritating when he corrected my grammar. If I were to make a grammatical mistake today, I wouldn't be much surprised if he sat up in his casket and corrected me. But I am grateful now for all of it. It has played a good part in who I am today.

I had wondered how sincere I could be in my tribute to him. I didn't feel much sadness, but I did realize I was speaking with full sincerity.

> The final thing I will say about his legacy to me is that it is a legacy of books. The reading of books—a fascination with the ideas and stories they contain. The worlds they open up. Especially the world of faith, of the

> Christian heritage. His books began that for me years ago. And now in these recent years that world is getting larger and larger as I roam the vast Christian tradition of the last two thousand years. I give thanks for this and honor him for this legacy.

He was laid to rest in the Allen plot of a cemetery just outside Russellville. I don't remember much about the graveside ceremony or the events that followed. The next day we flew back to Iowa and back to the studies.

I'm not proud to say that I've not missed him much. What I've missed was the father he wasn't. I missed his support—just his presence—throughout all my years of sports. I missed adventures together, laughter, and his showing me a pathway into the world of men. I missed his approval and his blessing. And more.

His mark on my life and career was strong—stronger than I've known, or at least stronger than I wanted to admit. He was the primary one who set in place the world I inherited and inhabited—and the world I've been striving for much of a lifetime to understand and expand.

CHAPTER 15

BELIEVING, TEACHING, AND PROFESSING

> "Doctrine is what the church of Jesus Christ believes, teaches, and confesses on the basis of the Word of God."
>
> —Jaroslav Pelikan

I remember vividly the very first time I stepped in front of a class of seminary students. I was a guest professor in the summertime, and it was pretty clear to me that it was a tryout situation. "Let's take a good look at this young theology guy," I think they were saying. And they did. I ended up joining the faculty the next academic year.

I was just coming off being a graduate student for nine years, and I still hadn't quite finished my dissertation. Along the way I had taught classes of undergraduates for five years as a graduate teaching assistant. But this was my first time to teach graduate students and to be entirely in charge of the class from beginning to end. It was exciting. And it was daunting. I remember thinking,

"What if they ask me questions I don't know how to answer?" And I remember being haunted for a couple of years by the feeling that I would be found out—discovered to be an imposter masquerading as a professor of theology. But I persisted, not shrugging off the fears but pressing through them and letting them move me to work very hard.

During these early years of teaching, we were thrilled to welcome two more children into our family: Daniel and, two years later, Bethany. Daniel, in contrast to the boldness of his older brother, David, was pensive, quiet, and reticent in conversations; but like his brother, he was curious and kind and always helpful. Bethany had an easy grace to her, loved her brothers dearly, and was quietly self-confident. We lived across the street from the university, and they loved to ride their cycles on the campus, occasionally join me for lunch in the cafeteria, and sometimes go for an evening swim with me in the campus pool.

All three attended our neighborhood public elementary school. There each of them, as part of the Accelerated Learning Program, participated in what we came to call the egg drop saga. In the third grade each was asked to take a raw egg and figure out a way to package it so that when it was dropped from the roof of the school building it wouldn't break.

David, our oldest, put his egg in Styrofoam packing peanuts. The egg broke. Several years later when it was his turn, Daniel used a section from an egg carton and packed confetti around it. His egg survived the drop, and he felt pretty proud. Bethany's turn came a couple of years later. She used cotton balls interspersed with cardboard squares. But the egg didn't survive the drop. When we expressed our sympathy that evening, she said, "That's okay. I'm actually glad it broke. Because if it hadn't, my friend Jessica would have been the only one whose egg broke."

All three had this kind of sensitivity to other children, and I was sometimes amazed at how it came out.

Daniel was our Hector the Collector (to borrow the title of a Shel Silverstein poem). As a small boy he developed the habit of scouring the ground wherever he was. We lived in the country for a few years, and there he found armadillo bones, bird skulls, snakeskins, an arrowhead, and, most of all, interesting rocks: fossils, geodes (which could be split open to expose crystals), water-polished rocks, igneous rocks, sandstone rocks. He loved rocks. Years later, when choosing a career, he chose petroleum geology, where for years now he's gotten to look at rocks most days, describing well cores and examining rock sections under an electron miscroscope.

Over these years I taught theology to scores of ministry students. Many of these students were members of—and some were already employed as ministers in—Churches of Christ. So a key aspect of my teaching was helping them locate themselves in the Christian tradition, realizing that, whether they knew it or not, they had been and were being shaped by a particular theological tradition. And that this location was not a bad thing, but just the place we find ourselves and out of which we work.

I found it helpful to compare learning Christian theology to learning a new language. Both involve a disciplined submission to a set of rules (a grammar), a new vocabulary, and a long tradition that carries forward a body of knowledge. In theology we begin learning the common language of faith. We learn Scripture and the history of its interpretation; the contours of the tradition as shaped by the creeds, catechisms, and classic doctrinal treatises;

and at least an outline of how the Christian church made its way through history. We enter humbly into worlds and ways of speaking not our own, and this long perspective shapes how we make it our own in our own time. If the goal of language learning is to speak confidently and effectively in that language, then the goal of theology learning is to speak and live out the way of Christ in the church and before the world.

As part of the framework for this, I would point students to the work of Jaroslav Pelikan, the greatest historian of Christian doctrine in the twentieth century. In a magisterial five-volume work, he sought to trace what the church "believed, taught, and confessed" over the centuries. He defined what is "believed" as the form of doctrine found in the literature of devotion and worship. What is "taught" was the content of Scripture extracted by exegesis and communicated through sermons and catechisms. And what is "confessed" was the church's testimony against false teaching and set forth in polemical writings and creeds.

I stressed that the form Christian doctrine has taken over the centuries is tradition. Tradition designates the handing down of Christian teaching. And dealing with tradition is inescapable. It is simply unavoidable that humans receive the witness of Scripture through a process of traditioning or handing down. Along the way, the church always faces the pull toward tradition*alism*—toward becoming, we might say, a fossil museum; but with the wisdom of the tradition itself as a guide, it serves to anchor and help sustain our mission under God as we face new times and challenges. For the record, my father would not have understood—or if he had, could not have accepted—such a view of tradition.

In the late 1980s I presented a paper at a national conference of professors of Bible and theology. The session of which I was a part focused on the history of the relationship between science and faith. The respondent to my paper and the two others was the eminent theologian Langdon Gilkey, who at that time was near the end of his career. He had long, gray and white hair, a gray beard, and wore a bright red scarf tied around his neck. From the printed program he could tell that I was from a Church of Christ-related university, so when we talked afterward, he asked me a few questions about that.

Then he wanted to tell me a story. He said that many years earlier a well-known leader in Churches of Christ—he called the man's name—had taken a doctoral course with him at Vanderbilt University Divinity School. It was a course on the history of theology in which they were reading works by Augustine of Hippo, one of the greatest of all Christian theologians: *Confessions*, excerpts from *On the Trinity* and *The City of God*, and other selections. After one of the classes, the Church of Christ leader came up to the professor and said something close to, "These writings by Augustine—I never knew how rich and insightful they are. They're amazing! Too bad he wasn't a true Christian."

Professor Gilkey laughed big at his own story, as if to say, "Of course, I know you don't share such an odd perspective as your older Church of Christ colleague."

In my theology classes over the years, I experienced something similar with students. I would assign excerpts from key shapers of the Christian tradition, ranging from Athanasius, Basil the Great, Augustine, Martin Luther, John Calvin, John Wesley, and Jonathan Edwards to Reinhold Niebuhr and Dietrich Bonhoeffer. Most of the students were from Churches of Christ and were being exposed to these writers for the first time. Occasionally, a student would come up to me during a break and say, "Dr. Allen, I'm just not sure how to think about Martin Luther. Do you think that Luther was really a Christian?" And I would say something like, "Well, you've read our selections from Luther—and you may want to read more than that. But given what you've read, why don't you try to answer that question for yourself?" That might lead, if we had time, into a longer conversation. Or it might end it for the time being.

I found inducting students into the Christian theological tradition to be a challenging and sometimes delicate process. My observation over many years was that the student response tended to fall into three types. First, and most common, was the experience of what I might call a joyous freedom, almost a sense of relief at getting oriented to a larger horizon on the Christian landscape. Second was the response that, though it may be good to know these things, it was mostly irrelevant to the commitment to restoring New Testament Christianity. And third was the response of a small number of students who became disoriented and troubled. I discerned that most of these students had been strongly indoctrinated into a very narrow Church of Christ world and—like me in some ways during my early years—didn't know what to do with it. What concerned me was that their world seemed to collapse rather than to enlarge. I tried to be especially sensitive to these students.

My basic introduction to theology course always had a big unit on the doctrine of the Trinity. I would declare to the students, from the beginning, that I was going to convince them that the doctrine of the Trinity, far from being an arcane and theoretical puzzle, was the centerpiece of Christian faith and eminently practical. That is to say, it shapes our practices as disciples and as a church. Near the end of the unit, I would usually ask the question: "If I were to wake you up at 3 a.m., shine a bright light in your eyes, and say to you, 'What is the meaning of the doctrine of the Trinity?' how would you answer?" [laughter] By that time, the students mostly would be able to answer something like: "The meaning of the doctrine of the

Trinity is that God is relational and that God is perfect love—that God not only seeks relationship with human creatures, but that God *is* a relationship: Father, Son, and Holy Spirit."

If I could turn them into full-fledged Trinitarians—the foundational doctrine of the Christian faith—I would view the course as a success.

CHAPTER 16

SOMETHING BETTER

> "The past is our definition. We may strive with good reason to escape it, or to escape what is bad in it. But we will escape it only by adding something better to it."
>
> —Wendell Berry

In 1988 I was one of a trio who wrote a small volume called *The Worldly Church*. It was what might best be called a "tract for the times," and it caused something of a furor for several years. It argued that Churches of Christ were inadvertently accommodating the secular spirit of the times with an emphasis on self-reliance and downplaying divine transcendence and the activity of the Holy Spirit. And the book called for a renewal of the heart of the gospel—the message of the cross—and for the church to become a community of the cross.

Two years later a more substantive follow-up book was released. It had an odd title: *The Cruciform Church*. When I was deciding whether or not to use this title, I asked a couple of friends what they thought. One said, "I don't think so. It's a new word for most people, and it will likely be off-putting." The other one reflected, "It could work. It would be risky, but it might be provocative enough to get people's attention." But from the beginning my wife said, "Yes! That's the word! That's *exactly* the right word." And, as it turned out, it was indeed the right word. The book got a strong reading, and *cruciform* became a new word in the vocabulary of many people.

This book took shape as a follow-up to several problems highlighted in *The Worldly Church*. One was the de-centering of the cross in the preaching in Churches of Christ in general.

A striking example of this de-centering appears in T. W. Brents's huge volume from 1847, *The Gospel Plan of Salvation*, a standard in the tradition for generations. I had first become familiar with this tome in the bookroom as a boy. It was hugely intimidating to me then. Only many years later—in the research leading up to *The Cruciform Church*—did I get a sense of its overall theology. It's a book of 662 pages, and its only extended treatment of Jesus's death is a five-page section devoted to refuting the Calvinist doctrine of limited atonement. Nowhere does one find any extensive or systematic discussion of human need and how God met that need in the cross of Jesus. The author devotes 306 pages to a discussion of baptism. But even there, I found only about two pages connecting baptism to the death of Christ. In a book claiming to set forth the gospel plan of salvation, I found such a ratio incomprehensible.

How could this happen? That's one of the conundrums I set out to explore in *The Cruciform Church*.

Here's the way I pieced together the answer. The movement had become preoccupied with form and structure and with setting in order what was lacking. The atonement was a classic Christian doctrine that almost everyone already believed. It didn't need to be defended or restored. It could be assumed. What needed restoring was the correct answer to the question, "What must I do to be saved?" What needed restoring was the "ancient order of things."

This approach to the atonement yielded two closely related problems. First, it tended to level the New Testament into a collection of doctrinal facts. Jesus's cross was one of these facts, important to be sure, but only one fact among many others in the New Testament pattern. Second, engaging the mysteries and profundities of the atonement held little practical value. The surpassing question was simply, "What are the steps to salvation?" The cross was an historical fact, and one must certainly believe the fact, but then the major focus fell on one's proper response to it.

To address this problem, *The Cruciform Church* (as the title suggests) set forth the centrality of the cross of Jesus for the life of the church. The "word of the cross" not only pervades the New Testament writings, but it provides the lens focusing the basic vision of what life in Christ should be like. It does this in three ways. First, the cross of Jesus reveals the heart—the passionate love—of God most clearly. Second, it reveals the depths of God's grace and of human sin. And third, the cross provides the model for God's alternative social order, calling us to take up the cross and seek to absorb hostility and abuse with forgiveness and peace. And so we are baptized into a community where living out the way of the cross begins to make sense in a world with a radically different vision of the good life.

A second problem in the tradition that I sought to address was what has sometimes been called "sectarian exclusivism" (although I didn't use that term). It's the assumption that Churches of Christ are the one true church, identical in every significant way to the church of the New Testament, and that all the denominations are hopelessly out of favor with God.

This perspective was a pervasive conviction in my world growing up—deeply assumed and mostly unquestioned. Ever since my early teens, it had troubled me. It marked one of my recurring big questions.

Years later I learned that the exclusive spirit began to emerge in Alexander Campbell's reform movement as soon as the 1830s. It remained a swelling stream among those who eventually became Churches of Christ. "I mean to say distinctly and emphatically," Moses Lard wrote in 1863, "that Martin Luther, if not immersed, was not a Christian. . . . I recognize no human being as a Christian who is not immersed." A late nineteenth-century Texas leader said, "We do not recognize Baptists as Christians, because they have not been baptized for the remission of sins." This view became dominant among Churches of Christ: everyone who had not submitted to proper baptism (as Churches of Christ have traditionally interpreted it) would be eternally lost, no matter how sincere their faith or how Christlike their lives.

To address this issue, *The Cruciform Church* recognized Churches of Christ as embedded in a real human tradition. And all human traditions have limitations, blindnesses; they sometimes misconstrue things—even the gospel. Some preachers began saying that the gospel required "minute conformity" as the basis for a person's relationship with God. In response, Mr. Campbell tried to arrest and correct this trajectory as early as 1837. He said that, if forced to choose between one who embraced what he viewed as the "essentials" and one who did not but was more "spiritually minded and devoted to the Lord," he would not hesitate "in giving the preference of my heart to the one that loveth most." The gospel calls people into a living relationship with God based on love, trust, and humble obedience.

For me, a significant marker on this journey occurred in my second year of doctoral studies. Holly and I had become friends with another doctoral student in theology and his wife: Bruce and Joan. Lovely people. We talked gardening and flowers. We talked about our children. We talked theology at a serious level. We talked about the two different paths that had formed us as Christians. They were from a Church of the Brethren heritage, a strict and robust Christian group with its own distinct history. We shared our history among Churches of Christ. They had hardly heard of it, and they were surprised by but very respectful of some of our distinctive beliefs and practices. We had in common a strong commitment to following Jesus focused around a classically orthodox theology. They had been expanding their horizons somewhat, just as we had been expanding ours.

The friendship with Bruce and Joan served as a significant marker for us. It dawned on us with some force that Bruce and Joan were fully Christian just as they were. We didn't need to convert them to anything or instruct them in the way of the Lord more perfectly. They were fine; indeed, they were exemplary. This possibility had been an abstract idea for some time. But with Bruce and Joan it took on actual flesh.

The de-centering of the cross and the strong spirit of sectarian exclusivism were two theological viewpoints that troubled me as a young adult. *The Cruciform Church* was my attempt to move past them and into something better.

CHAPTER 17

DESERT ECOLOGY

> "Gardens are about waiting and about hope as much as they are about anything. Spring comes when it comes; roses bloom when they will. What it teaches you is to wait, to be patient, and to pay attention."
>
> —Robert Benson

About fifteen years into my academic career, a personal crisis precipitated in me what I might call a spiritual collapse. It would fit under the umbrella of what John of the Cross famously called a dark night of the soul. There are various species of that genus; mine had deep roots in my past—in the very story I've given a few glimpses into here. Driven, perfectionistic, a bit of a savior complex, but always the nice guy; I couldn't carry it anymore.

The crisis unfolded in stages over a period of several years. It included several complex dimensions—bouts of dark depression, a private misunderstanding with a colleague, the political and emotional pressures of leading a controversial church plant, and wrongdoing in my own life. Things finally broke in a perfect storm as my own private woes hit the rocks of a church's public turmoil. The church broke up. Lots of people were devastated. I found myself both offended and offender, wronged and wrongdoer. I abruptly resigned my university teaching post right before the beginning of a new academic year and retreated to my own desert.

Deserts are tough places to live. Survival requires special adaptation to extreme temperatures and arid conditions. The danger of heat-induced dehydration makes deserts dangerous places. Desert mammals, like camels, can maintain body temperatures that are about equal to typical desert air temperatures. This adaptation allows them to retain large amounts of water for extended periods of time. Other desert dwellers tend to become nocturnal and live mostly in burrows underground. The desert has its own harsh ecology.

So I found myself living in a desert. A desert of the heart and spirit—deadly and full of dangers in its own way. Casting my eyes over the empty and unfamiliar vista before me, I wondered how I could adapt to such extreme conditions.

I had loved gardening since I was a boy. I thought back to my boyhood, to Winter Garden, where flowers and vegetables of all sorts grew year-round. The giant poinsettia and hibiscus and croton bushes. The Japanese plum. The tangerine and kumquat trees in the backyard. The vegetable garden of my early years had always remained vivid in my imagination. Pulling big carrots and onions out of the sandy loam. Cutting cabbages and kohlrabi. Selling vegetables to my parents for our dinner table. I associated it all with productivity and peacefulness. And over the years since, wherever I had a little patch of dirt, I would usually plant a few vegetables and flowers. In a couple of those early gardens, my oldest son, David, as a preschool boy, was my always eager helper.

Now I had half an acre—and more. And I had all the time in the world, with nowhere to go, except driving the children to and from school.

I decided to grow a garden. A big one, a garden in the desert.

I began the flowerbed in early January. I marked out a five-feet by thirty-feet bed along the south side of our house, and I began digging it by hand. I first removed a thick layer of St. Augustine grass, and then, step-by-step, hour by hour, spaded the soil a foot deep. It took days and left my hands blistered. It was exhausting and felt really good.

Following my careful blueprint, I planted an array of spring bulbs first. Then, weeks later, I planted seedlings that had been growing inside under lights: Shasta daisies, zinnias, marigolds, black-eyed Susans, snapdragons, and sunflowers. And I planted what turned into an amazing butterfly bush. The butterfly bush had arrived in the mail and was just a bare and dead-looking root about eight inches long. The catalog had said "bareroot," but I hadn't expected it to be that bare.

When the first wave of planting was all done it looked like . . . nothing—just a long strip of bare ground. When the second wave was done ten weeks later—the perennial and annual seedlings—it still looked puny and pitiful, with no hint of any future glory. But I knew different. I had done this before.

The vegetable garden was next. From a friend who lived about ten miles away I borrowed an old tractor with what I think was called a three-disc bedder plow. It took several hours but I ended up with a sandy half-acre field mostly ready for planting. I put a light wire fence all around it and then laid out a drip irrigation system with tubes and drip holes, including a fertilizing canister hooked into the system. Over several weeks I planted in stages: turnips, broccoli, black-eyed peas, green beans, okra, squash, watermelon, and various kinds of pepper and tomato plants. And onions—I set out a thousand plants of a sweet variety called Texas 1015.

I pumped all of this with liquid fertilizer through the drip system every two to three weeks. I watched things grow day by day, constraining my impatience and eagerness and hoping for the best. The garden gradually filled out, the vegetables swelling right before my eyes. A little excitement began to rise each day.

And I began to notice that some rabbits were casing the garden, apparently sharing my excitement. One day I saw a couple of very young rabbits nosing around. I thought to myself, "This is not your buffet. Please leave." I ran into the house and picked up my son's BB gun, thinking I would simply scare them away. I took aim at one and fired. It was a good thirty yards away. To my surprise and chagrin the BB hit it in the head, in the one vulnerable spot, and the little rabbit flipped up in the air and fell still to the ground. I had killed Thumper.

Rabbits notwithstanding, I enjoyed a bumper crop. Bushels of peppers, beans, squash, okra. And especially onions—softball-size onions, sweet as could be. I had large boxes full of onions sitting around the garage for months. Only the tomatoes were meager—the summer heat, often over a hundred degrees, had been too much for them.

And it wasn't many weeks until the flowers began to make a grand entrance. A cacophony of colors: purples, yellows, white, red, pink, and a few blues. And a butterfly bush, covered in lavender blooms, that grew to six feet in one season.

What to do with all the vegetables? I soon hit on the answer: the downtown farmers' market. After checking it out and learning how it worked, I showed up my first Saturday morning with several big boxes of vegetables. Most farmers, I noticed, sold their produce in small one-dollar baskets. I joined them, and I think I made close to a hundred dollars that first morning. For the rest of the summer and into the fall I set up at the market on Tuesdays and Saturdays, harvesting the evening before and hitting the road at 6 a.m. for the market eight miles away. The onions were a steady hit all summer. I finally sold all of them by early September.

Daniel and Bethany sometimes joined me at the market—as they often did in the garden. They loved the adventure of it—telling about our garden, learning how to deal with customers, answering questions about the produce, and handling sales.

Through the four to five months of the growing season, we earned enough to pay our house payment each month. I did the garden and the market again the next year, and the crops again were bountiful. But near the end of the second season my family and I moved to Southern California for Holly to complete her doctorate at a seminary. We sold our house and left the garden behind.

The desert season wasn't over; as it turned out, it was still in the early stages. Growing a garden was a survival occupation. It held me; it held the beckoning abyss at bay. I was learning some of the ways of desert life, some of the survival skills. I was slowly learning "to wait, to be patient, and to pay attention."

CHAPTER 18

DESERT PREOCCUPATIONS

> "It's hard to know what to do with your emptiness when you're not supposed to have emptiness."
>
> —Miriam Toews

In Southern California the barrenness of the desert continued to loom large. It was no mirage. What does one do in the desert besides mitigate the heat (and cold) and forage for survival? My vocational capital was all in the academy. I had put in my ten thousand hours in research and writing and through fifteen years in the university classroom. My books had found a strong readership for a decade. What might one do with such a résumé in the emptiness of the desert?

Somehow—I don't remember exactly how—the idea of publishing books pertaining to Churches of Christ and their history emerged. It was a presumptuous and daunting idea, but that did not stop two colleagues and close friends from jumping on it, insisting that "You are just the person to do that, and this is just the season for it." I didn't have much else to do, truth be told; and my ignorance of what it would take to enter that complex, multidimensional world prevented me from seeing many red flags.

From my makeshift office in one corner of the garage in our little rental house in Southern California, I took the leap. It was a big leap. One starts, I supposed, with some ideas for a few books. Which I had. And then with a modest strategic plan—for editing, book production, book manufacturing, and for promoting and selling the books. Not to mention financing the operation and learning the legal ropes of incorporation, author contracts, and royalties.

I jumped into a dozen or so learning curves all at once. And as time passed, the curves got steeper. From desktop publishing technology to book and cover design to the world of book manufacturing (these were the days before print-on-demand) to the hurdles involved in entering the book trade. Daunting, to the say the least. Then, even more challenging, the delicacies of manuscript acquisition and the technicalities of editing—from developmental editing to content editing to line editing and copyediting to proofreading. All intensive and meticulous.

I forged ahead. The first book was a new edition of a little-known spiritual classic from the mid-nineteenth century: *Communings in the Sanctuary* by Robert Richardson, a collection of talks delivered around the Lord's table in the Bethany Church of Christ. For years I had wanted to see a new edition of the long out-of-print book, first published in the 1850s. I wrote a substantial theological introduction and then typed the old book into a Word file. A graphic designer friend taught me how to use QuarkXPress, with which I typeset the book and designed the cover. I had a thousand copies printed and launched my first title.

It was a risk, though not a huge one. I had borrowed money from three investors. I needed to sell hundreds of this book. To my surprise, I did. A steady stream of books followed: I think I published five the first year, then maybe eight the second, and gradually a few more each year.

The first couple of years I wore all the hats and did all the jobs. I acquired manuscripts, edited first drafts, proofread every page, advertised, took orders, managed the finances, warehoused the books, packed the books, and shipped the books. My garage was the first warehouse. I was constantly learning, upgrading, and expanding my knowledge of the publishing landscape. I began to experiment with freelance editors, cover designers, book designers, and manufacturers, and gradually, over three or four years, I developed a publishing team.

From the beginning, this venture filled my life with an intensity that was all-encompassing. It was not always healthy. But as a desert preoccupation, it kept the withering heat and emptiness—sometimes the despair—at bay. It gave me good work to do, work that drew upon my scholarly pedigree and academic reputation.

The venture succeeded beyond my founding hopes and dreams. I paid off the loan in year two. The growing sales gave me adequate working capital for new titles, along with a small income. I was hoping to see a book take off in sales; that didn't happen, but several sold very well for a new press working in a niche market. In year five I sold my little publishing company to a university press that had been languishing; the sale was contingent on me becoming director of the new combined entity. I agreed and was glad to begin receiving a full-time salary.

The new institutional affiliation provided more resources for expansion and for gaining recognition for the press. I began developing several new lines of books: titles about and for Christian higher education, titles for the general Christian trade, titles on the history and theology of the Stone–Campbell Movement / Churches of Christ, and titles on the history and culture of the region around the university. I began networking widely with leaders in Christian universities that were members of the Council for Christian Colleges & Universities. And I led the press through the rigorous process of becoming a member of the Association of American University Presses (now the Association of University Presses). Sales quadrupled, and the staff expanded to eight people.

For fourteen years book publishing was my occupation and preoccupation, the first seven or eight of those years in the desert. It filled the emptiness, but more than that, this enterprise introduced me to the rigors, risks, and exhausting, never-ending, dawn-to-dusk working world of the small-business owner. I took my humble place in the long line of those who sell their wares. For years I drove our little Ford Ranger to regional and national gatherings, setting up my booth, selling books.

And along the way, in this desert, God began a new work in me.

CHAPTER 19

DESERT WELLS

> "In the deserts of the heart
> Let the healing fountain start,
> In the prison of his days
> Teach the free man how to praise."
> —W. H. Auden (1940)

Early on in the desert season, my wife Holly wrote me a long letter. It was near the lowest point in my desert sojourn. "Though you find it almost impossible to believe," she began, "God really loves you, C. Leonard Allen. He saw and knew you when you were a little boy trying so hard to be perfect. He loved you then; he loves you now. God loves you like we love David, Daniel, and Bethany, not because they are wise and perfect. We love them as they are but also for who they will be. We love them and teach them and see them grow and rejoice with them. God loves us that way."

The letter continued: "God desires for you to use again the good gifts he has given you. In the past he has used you to construct bridges for people, and they have walked happily over those bridges to a freer place in Christ where they breathe in his Spirit with lighter hearts. But somehow what you did for others, you could not do for yourself."

Near the end she said: "God desires for you to be whole and healed. The wounds that are open and gaping and so vulnerable to re-wounding will close; they will heal. You will be able to stand upright; you will be able to walk about without pain. God has made us so that we heal."

During the Israelites' desert wanderings, the book of Numbers notes that they came to a place called Be'er ("well" in Hebrew), where they discovered a well. In the middle of the desert, it was an unexpected source of water—an unexpected source of hope, sustenance, and healing. There at Be'er, "Israel sang this song: 'Spring up, O well! Sing about it'" (Num. 21:17).

Deserts are tough places to live. But good things can happen there if we can adapt to the severe conditions and pay attention. For me, the desert, over a long stretch of years, eventually became a healing place. In our small California rental house, I began the journey back to life.

One turning point happened at a two-day retreat with a spiritual director in the Northwest. On the afternoon of day two, while I was resting on the bed but not asleep, I experienced something entirely new in my life—a dreamlike scene of the utmost vividness:

> From a bird's-eye vantage point I saw a rock quarry—somewhat like the one I had seen years earlier at Mauthausen, the Austrian World War II concentration camp.
>
> Then the view slowly drew down into the quarry, so that I could begin to see a small boy looking up at

me. As my view came closer, I could see that he was dressed in Sunday clothes, hair neatly combed, his face plaintively peering upward. His hands were holding something, and he slowly raised it, offering it to me as I approached. It was a small glass vial containing a cloudy liquid. Dirty water.

It hit me: the little boy had been laboring to extract water from the stones, and now with a sweet and earnest face he was offering it to me. And I could now see his face. It was me.

I didn't know what to call that experience. I still don't. All I know is that I wept and wept over the hours, days, even weeks that followed—tears of release, tears of compassion, tears of healing.

"Spring up, O well!"

There were other unexpected water sources as the journey continued, mostly in the form of unlikely people who, without much reason (that I could see), came alongside me. There was the businessman in Costa Mesa who latched onto me when I wandered into a spiritual formation group. He simply would not let me stay away. He called me over and over, insisting that I enter fully into the disciplines of the group. I did, reluctantly, and stuck with it for over two years. There were others—a cheery commercial real estate salesman who embraced me and began to teach me how the world works, a university professor well down the road from his own deep crisis who invited me to join him on his return path, and a few others.

"Spring up, O well!"

The desert wells were few and far between. Lots of things get lost and stripped away in the desert. Things that once seemed impressive and important wither and blow away. The simplicity and starkness of the desert reduce one to bare essentials—and it comes as somewhat of a surprise to learn just what those essentials are and what one can live without.

Something else about the desert: in the desert one may become other. The realm of the other is the place across that big divide where, formerly, we looked over and occasionally saw those broken and pitiable ones, the shameful, unpresentable, or scandalous ones. The ones outside the camp. The others. In the desert, one may begin to see oneself as other. And as that happens, the world begins to look different. Indeed, the whole world changes.

During the long desert journey I was not literally alone. Holly, who was completing her PhD dissertation and teaching at a Christian university, loved me hard and loved me well all along the way. During a couple of these years I was a visiting professor at the same university, and my book publishing enterprise with its huge learning curves was a consuming preoccupation. Our two younger children were completing high school, and I went to baseball games, track meets, tennis matches, school programs, conferences, and other special events.

But the desert remained the dominant reality. I did eventually emerge from it, though precisely when that was I can't say. And when I did, I found myself a different person. To tell that part of the story, I will use two new metaphors: climbing a new mountain and learning to dance.

CHAPTER 20

THE SECOND MOUNTAIN

> "They say nothing is my fault, and I wish they wouldn't say that. How can a man be forgiven if nothing is his fault?"
>
> —Miriam Toews

Some people's lives are a two-mountain journey. The first mountain is the climb to make something of oneself—to establish one's own identity apart from parents, to establish a family and a career, to gain a reputation through one's work and accomplishments, to become well-respected and build a secure ego. It's the mountain many of us start climbing almost without thinking about it.

But somewhere along the way, for a variety of reasons, some of us find ourselves in the valley beyond that mountain. Some crisis, some soul-crushing anguish draws one—sometimes hurtles one—down the mountain and into the valley below. And there, in that valley, can begin, David Brooks says (and indeed, deep Christian wisdom says), a three-step process: "Dying to the old self, cleansing in the emptiness, resurrecting in the new."

The first step is a coming undone. The second is a move into the desert, a place of barrenness where things get stripped away. In the desert one is forced to confront one's life at the deepest and truest level. "When you get down to the core of yourself," says Brooks, "you find a different, more primeval country, and in it a deep yearning to care and connect." There in the desert, usually after a good long sojourn, one begins to discern the outlines of the second mountain, a bigger and very different mountain.

When I found myself in the valley below and around the first mountain, something most unexpected occurred. Two people found me there. We had been acquaintances for some years, and we had admired each other, mostly from afar. But that year they reached out, and we began to form a circle of friendship.

The personal crisis I mentioned in the previous three chapters was just unfolding. I had resigned my teaching post and retreated to my own wilderness. I remember vividly the day these two men invited me to one of their homes and asked me to tell my story. I didn't know how to proceed at first. To clear a space for me to ease into, one of them told some of his own story—of a season years before when he had experienced a deep betrayal followed by a long journey of recovery and reorientation.

This was a strange new place for me, one I had not visited before. To be received there by two people who knew the place seemed unbelievable. I began to tell my story, haltingly at first and then in a torrent. In the weeks and months that followed, the three of us went around the circle and back again, telling our stories with richer texture and greater forthrightness.

And so began our long friendship journey. Their friendship became a sustaining presence. It helped me survive the barren terrain and, eventually, to begin to see the fogged contours of the second mountain.

The bond that formed among the three of us was built around candor, trust, common interests, joint adventures, easy presence, and—as we gradually discovered—similar experiences with our fathers. Each of us had longed to be known, affirmed, and blessed by a father who had been largely unable to do that.

For most of these years the three of us have lived in different parts of the country. But the friendship has remained strong and steady, marked and sustained by certain practices and rhythms. One key practice is a commitment to getting together for a retreat one, two, even three times a year. The three of us have climbed mountains, hiked forests, walked beaches, explored wine countries, discovered urban centers, and hidden out in out-of-the-way cabins. Wherever we are, we enact a kind of ritual: a circling back in some way to our stories—well-known to each other—to catch up on unfolding episodes, to explore continuing challenges, and to assess and bless.

We live in different spheres, face different pressures, have other friends. The level of regular contact ebbs and flows. But we seem always to pick up where we left off—knowing and being known, trusting and being trusted, loving and being loved. We are friends. We know each other's stories intimately, and we hold them as a sacred trust. And we have good evidence that our friendship radiates beyond ourselves to bless our wives, our children, and others who know us as leaders and friends.

I think I can say that our friendship, for me, has been an adventure between two mountains. It began in a deep valley below the first mountain and has sustained us, each in our own way, through an expanse of desert; and it continues to enable us as we journey on that second mountain. It's the place where we begin to discover that truer, better self, that more primordial country, a place where we yearn to connect more with others, to give more to others. It is the place from which I have been able to attend more closely to my children and to seek their forgiveness for my early neglect and the tidal wave I brought on them. Second-mountain life, David Brooks says, "is a life of love, care, and commitment. It is the antidote to much that is wrong in our culture."

Over twenty-five years, our friendship has continued and grown. Across the expanse of great distances. Through strong vocational and life pressures. Through sorrows and losses. Through seasons of disorientation and momentous life decisions.

We make no extravagant claims for our friendship, but I do claim that it has done much to help us, each in our own way, press into life on the second mountain. And to be clear, second-mountain life, I think, is but another way of speaking of the self-surrendering way of Jesus.

CHAPTER 21

DANCING LESSONS

> "Dance me through the panic till I'm gathered safely in
> Lift me like an olive branch and be my homeward dove
> Dance me to the end of love."
>
> —Leonard Cohen

The desert sojourn lasted several years. I did eventually emerge from it—and when I did I found myself a different person. To tell that part of the story I will use a fourth metaphor.

Let me say that I began—awkwardly, of course—learning to dance.

This is certainly an odd image for a good Church of Christ boy. All through the elementary years I sat out every single square dance at my school, and all through high school and college I never attended a single dance. I had been taught since childhood that all dancing was off-limits for true Christians. I even got the impression that fornication was forbidden because it could lead to dancing. As an adult, the very muscles in my legs seemed to be wired with a deep inhibition against it.

The first time I ever stepped on a dance floor was when I escorted my lovely and graceful high school daughter, Bethany, to the annual father–daughter banquet. There, to my embarrassment, I found myself out on the dance floor with her trying to move my body to the sounds of that classic song "Who Let the Dogs Out." Not an enviable sight!

But I've slowly been learning to dance. I don't mean physically, though that is a good thing. I mean with myself. I mean with God.

For a long season I joined a small group of people for a midday, midweek communion service. One week when I entered the room, I saw on a tripod near the lectern an oversize replica of Andrei Rublev's famous icon of the Trinity (1425). I knew it well. It depicts the three angels who visited Abraham and Sarah to announce the birth of Isaac (Gen. 18). But those three angels also portray in a profound way the three members of the Trinity. Their faces are bent toward each other; you can see their self-effacing love for one another, and their eyes are full of enjoyment.

As I gazed on it before the service began, I found myself deeply moved. And a bit later while the leader spoke briefly about the picture—and the life of the painter—two things dawned on me. First: the theological and spiritual revolution that is the Christian vision of the Trinity had been the biggest and most profound *theological* discovery on my journey; it had been a net beneath me, holding me and preserving my faith all those years ago. And second: in the desert years, it had held me against the strong allure of the abyss, the desire simply not to be.

What made all the difference for me was beginning to see the *function* of Trinitarian doctrine. Or to put it better, the *nature* of Trinitarian life. For me this recast, even revolutionized, my understanding of what it means to be a Christian.

This theological recentering happened in the early years of my teaching, long before the desert season. Over those years I stressed to my students that the doctrine of the Trinity is not about some strange heavenly arithmetic. It is simply a shorthand way of referring to what we know of God now that Jesus—God incarnate—has come and the Holy Spirit has been poured out. God leads a relational life as Father, Son, and Spirit. That life is characterized by submissive love, as each pours life and love into the other. So abundant is this life that it overflows, and we are invited to share in it. So wonderful and rich that joy permeates it. And so perfect that it reaches down into our very deepest desires. Call it Trinitarian life. Call it Christian life.

As Diogenes Allen put it, "The life of the Trinity is a perfect community and it is the kind of community for which we long; it satisfies our craving to be loved perfectly and to be attached to others properly." This is what we seek above all in this life: the giving and receiving of love. Perfect love. We hardly know how to speak of that—or even to recognize it. Yet the living God invites us to partake of that life—the very life of the Trinity.

It is an invitation to dance. For many years I could speak with some profundity and not a little passion—and maybe a little eloquence—about that great dance. But, as my father had well taught me long ago, I was not allowed to dance. Even as I would hear the music and long to step into the rhythms, my feet would tangle and my heart would shrink. Was I a cripple? Was I ashamed? Was I unworthy?

For these past couple of decades I have been learning to dance. A good many years ago, I gave Holly dancing lessons as a birthday gift. Country dancing—the two-step. I of course had to go too, since she needed a partner. It looked easy enough, I thought. Who could mess up two steps? I quickly learned there was a lot more to it than two steps. There was knowing which way to turn, how to swing her around in various ways, when to go backward, and when forward. We eventually did some serious boot-scooting around that big floor. It was frustrating. And it was exhilarating. But through it all I just couldn't seem to get the inhibitions fully worked out of my muscles.

Learning to dance is quiet and slow, often awkward, rarely elegant. But the deep and joyful rhythms of grace sound loud and clear, and I'm stepping out with them. I keep training my legs (kneeling is good) and limbering my arms (gesturing is good) and lifting my heart (confessing the faith is good) and joining with beloved brothers and sisters (friendship is good).

The desert season remains an important and ever-present marker. I consider it a dark and necessary grace—though it took me a good many years to acknowledge that. The truth is that "grace is not gentle or made-to-order. It often comes disguised as loss, or failure, or unwelcome change." In Scripture deserts are places of testing, refining, and preparing. And so it was for me.

About eight years into the desert season, I began to realize that the season was receding. "My life, and that of my family, is on a firm and good path," I wrote to a former colleague. "Indeed, I am feeling freer and more peaceful than I can remember ever feeling. My creativity runs freer. My spirit runs freer. New friendships are flourishing. New insights—into myself and many other things—are flowing."

I was emerging into a new and surprising era in my life, moving into a kind of intense and creative work that I had not imagined.

One sign that I was coming out of the desert was my agreement to teach a Sunday adult class at our large church. I was surprised at myself for agreeing. It was a seven-week series, and I titled it "How the Doctrine of the Trinity Keeps the Christian Life on Track."

In the promotional description, I wrote: "In the early church the Trinitarian vision of God was central for Christian identity, worship, and discipleship. For many Christians today, however, the Trinity is viewed as unreasonable, impractical, and mostly irrelevant. What exactly is the doctrine of the Trinity and why is it so central to the Christian faith? And how does it serve to keep the Christian life on track?"

On my way to the first class that Sunday morning, I wondered if anyone would come. To my surprise, a lot of people showed up. I don't recall ever having a more engaged and eager group of class members in a church. They didn't know they were signing up for some dancing lessons, but I think we all learned a few new moves. And for me, it marked the season I came back to life as a teacher of the Christian faith.

III

INTERLUDE

CHAPTER 22

COFFEE, BELATED

> "Oh, the hours I've spent in coffee shops, reading and writing."
>
> —Unknown

I completed two long graduate degrees—a three-year master's degree and a six-year doctorate—without coffee. I pulled all-nighters without coffee. I wrote a four-hundred-page dissertation over two years without coffee. I worked a night shift as a security guard—no coffee. I wrote several academic books over the next decade—no coffee. I spent a sabbatical semester in Vienna and learned about the important role of coffee shops in Viennese culture. But no coffee. It seems unbelievable, I know. But it's true.

Coffee remained a foreign substance to me for many years. I came to appreciate—even enjoy—its smell, but the dark liquid never crossed my lips. I never considered it an option—not because I had any big objection but just because I felt no need or desire for it. I knew nothing of its lore and complexities, much less the existence of those creatures sometimes called coffee snobs. I was a teenager when Alfred Peet's pioneering shop was established in Berkeley (1966). Then the new coffee culture exploded as the Starbucks chain began its meteoric rise (1971) toward its current thirty-six thousand shops. But it didn't touch me at all.

I drank coffee for the first time in a coffee shop in Siloam Springs, Arkansas, right after we moved from Orange County, California. I had begun my small book publishing company three years earlier, and when I moved it to this small, quaint Northwest Arkansas town, something almost magical happened. I was curious about coffee shop culture, and I didn't want to do my editorial work all alone at home. So I found myself in a small coffee shop called Pour Jons in an historic building in downtown Siloam Springs. I began working there two to three hours most weekdays. And I found myself drinking coffee—every day.

And I realized that I liked it. Not loved it, mind you. But liked it. Especially in wintertime. What I loved was the coffee shop atmosphere. A place where the other patrons, like me, had work to do, people to call or meet, emails to write. I had never used a public space like that before. The closest thing to it would have been my study carrel in the University of Iowa library. Soon I found myself nodding to the regulars, then smiles and warm greetings. Occasionally there would be brief get-acquainted or catch-up conversations. I remember the day that first year—it was Ash Wednesday—when the rector from the local Anglican church spent an hour in the shop anointing people with what he called "ashes to go."

And there was the morning sometime later when a precocious three-year-old with her grandparents sat down at a nearby booth with their bagels, milk, and coffee. The little girl had long, shoulder-length curls; an eager, excited face; and busy hands that, when they were not tearing off a piece of bagel to stuff in her mouth, were waving up and down to the background music.

The grandfather was a large man with a round, puffy face and short gray beard, a ring in one ear, and long sandy hair graying at the temples. For no reason, the little girl turned to him and said, "I love you, Grandpa!" He smiled, of course, and helped her spread more butter on the bagel. She then placed a plastic replica of a small votive candle in the middle of the table. It had a lighted plastic flame. She stood up in her seat and with delight announced to everyone, "We're having a celebration!"

It was a moment worth showing up for.

My taste for and knowledge of coffee steadily grew. I began to develop a taste for *good* coffee. To learn the basic options and possibilities. But not too fancy and not sweet. And definitely not iced. Or turned into some kind of coffee-flavored milkshake. But not a snob. Just a novice who was learning to appreciate and enjoy good coffee.

Something happened about five years into my coffee journey that made me realize how far I'd come. My daughter was studying and working in China, and she invited my wife and me to visit. She spoke Mandarin Chinese and would be our special tour guide.

A major stop on our ten-day tour was Xi'an. We had arrived on a fourteen-hour overnight train from Beijing. The long train was packed and, as far as I could tell, we were the only Westerners on board. We had sleeping berths, but the chorus of snoring from other passengers had made sleep fitful. We had arrived about 7 a.m. to join the throngs of people jamming the main station just outside the ancient wall of the city.

After breakfast and a nap at our hotel, we set off to the Shaanxi History Museum, recognized as the finest in China. Then, after a quick dinner of kebabs at a sidewalk café in the Muslim district, we hit the beds early.

At 4:30 the next morning I was awake for the day, my back stiff from the hard bed. Holly and Bethany thought they could sleep some more, so I left to give them quiet. I sat in the hotel lobby reading a John le Carré novel.

At 7 a.m., when the complimentary breakfast opened, I ate. It was a sight to see: a buffet of fried rice, steamed bread, congee (rice porridge), boiled eggs, tofu, stir-fried bok choy, and other plant material I didn't recognize. The food was abundant and good, but it felt like having a large and exotic Chinese dinner for breakfast.

After breakfast I continued the exploring I had begun the previous evening. Given to turning into out-of-the-way passageways, I had followed some strange smells down an alley and found the most exotic market I'd ever seen. There were live fish of all types in tanks and pools, live bullfrogs, snails, manta rays, and eels. And these were just the creatures I could recognize—many more I had never seen before, and some I had never envisioned as edible. The smells were thick and many-layered. Dozens of young men with carts and bicycles were hustling about delivering the delicacies.

What I wanted, I realized, was a brief respite from it all. I'm about as adventurous and bold as anyone, I daresay, but this morning—at the halfway point of our ten-day trip—I wanted a break. Something familiar and easy. Just for a little while.

I had seen the place the day before near the Muslim market, only a few blocks from our hotel. Retracing my path, I found it. It had not been a mirage. Starbucks. Yes!

The Chinese barista greeted me warmly—and he spoke good English. He prepared me a tall mug of their bold, organic Sumatra blend. I added whole milk—which I had not seen anywhere on the trip—and made my way to a table. The only other customers were an older American couple, and they smiled at me warmly and knowingly as I sat down. The Internet connection was simple and strong, and I caught up on three days of email as I drank my coffee.

Light rain was falling as I returned to the hotel to meet Holly and Bethany for our excursion to the terra cotta warriors. I thought to myself: "That was the best cup of coffee ever."

In my belated embrace of coffee, I had come a long way.

IV

RETRIEVALS

CHAPTER 23

THE QUALITY OF MERCY

> "Most of my regrets are failures to be kind or merciful. What haunts me most are people I loved who needed more mercy than I could or would give."
>
> —Russell Moore

Some years ago I was walking one foggy afternoon on a beach near San Diego with a pastor named Ken Blue. He had authored a book on spiritual abuse, and I was asking him questions about his experience with this widespread phenomenon. He was often called in by churches to deal with abusive leadership practices. He said that as he spoke at conferences over the years, he had been dismayed at how many spiritual abuse stories people wanted to share with him. In recent years, he confessed, he had struggled to fight despair over how widespread it appeared to be.

I asked him how he defined spiritual abuse. Most simply, he said, it happens when religious leaders with power use that power to coerce, control, or exploit a follower. It can be relatively mild, at one end of the spectrum, and at the other end, it can be heavy-handed and deeply abusive. And much of it, Ken said, is not done with intent to harm.

My meeting with him came in the aftermath of a troubling episode I had witnessed. A young woman in her early thirties—I'll call her Jenny—had been humiliated by and finally cast out of a church that she deeply loved. Her husband, a staff member of the church, had confessed—first to her, then to the church leaders—an improper relationship and publicly repented. But his repentance had been judged insincere by the leaders and rejected. He was put out of fellowship. And because Jenny didn't also reject his repentance, she too was removed from the church community. A letter was read to the church naming them both.

She was devastated. Uncomprehending. When my wife and I went to see her, her eyes seemed glassy, her voice listless, her body hardly moving. We sat with her a good while, not speaking.

Finally, gathering some words, Holly said simply, "We heard what happened. We wanted to come and tell you that we're so very sorry."

I knew Jenny had been schooled on Jesus since she was a small child. Jesus gentle and lowly. Friend of sinners. Shepherd of lost sheep.

She sat on the floor with her knees pulled up almost to her chin, rocking slowly forward and backward, eyes closed. What could I say? "Please know that Holly and I love you. And we can hardly bear to see you hurting like this." An almost imperceptible smile touched her lips, and her head began nodding slightly in rhythm with her rocking.

We said a few more things and then sat with her in silence for several more minutes.

"Thank you," she said softly after a while. "Thank you for coming. Means a lot." Holly touched her arm lightly, carefully, and we left her there on the floor, still rocking, and stepped out onto the front porch to leave.

I was angrier than I could remember being in a long time.

It was a long road for Jenny. Recovery was slow. A few close friends walked steadily with her, and a season of therapy helped. Her husband joined her, and together they brought their lives together again. Their beloved church became a bittersweet—and dangerous—memory.

I think Dallas Willard was right: in our spiritual growth, "we have to start from woundedness." This woundedness comes from deep injuries in our relationships with others. And it has two basic sources: lovelessness (in the form of assault or attack) and lack of proper care (resulting from withdrawal or distancing). Lovelessness works through a pattern of assault and withdrawal. This pattern becomes deeply embedded in our souls. It gets lodged in our memory where it threatens to shape our identity and cast a dark shadow over all we think and do. These memories tend to drag on our spirit like a ball and chain on a prisoner's leg. They constrict us, sometimes paralyze us, holding us back from joy, growth, and mature discipleship.

The healing of this woundedness—and the heavy memory of it—is profoundly social. God made us relational beings. That is to say, God made us in God's own image. God's own self is relational: a family of perfect love that we call the Trinity. The heart of Christian faith is that God invites us, draws and welcomes us, into that perfect society of love.

God does this supremely though the crucified One, who took upon himself the wrongs and sufferings of all—both wrongdoers and the wounded victims of wrongdoing. Christ took away the sin of the world (John 1:29), including the sins of those who have inflicted wrong and those who have suffered wrong. Indeed, we have all inflicted wrongs and suffered wrongs, often in one and the same relationship.

By Christ's unconditional mercy we receive forgiveness. And more: we begin to learn to imitate, in our own very human way, this forgiveness toward those who have wronged us. Thus we enter into Christ's new realm of love where we can experience forgiveness and the disruption of the deep pattern of woundedness in our lives.

We experience this love through the Holy Spirit and in and through the body of Christ in which the Spirit dwells. It becomes healing balm.

And sometimes it's tough medicine. The Spirit pours God's love into our hearts and brings us into union with Christ. But that's not a simple work. It often involves a "put[ting] to death" in our lives (Rom. 8:13). There is a dying to the old life, which was "according to the flesh"; the Spirit enables this putting-to-death process.

I've learned to view the desert season of my life in this way. It was a season when I was forced to come to the end of myself. It was a grace, but it was not of my choosing. Things got stripped away and burned up. I crossed over into the realm of the other, and when I did, the world forever changed. I changed. I can best call it a season of deep healing.

Here are some of the things that deep healing has meant for me and for my life in the decades since. First, I live these years out of a congruent self. The inner life and the outer are in sync—that is, what you see is mostly what you get. Second, I've learned to carry things with a kind of lightness—not all the time, but much of the time. I take my vocation with great seriousness and I work very hard at it, but it is not my life. It is not who I am. Third, I have learned to laugh—at myself, at the strange twists and turns of life in this world, and at the unexpected oddities of grace.

Fourth, I take joy in lifting up and promoting the work of others. I served as a book editor and publisher for over a decade, and that's what an editor does—attempt to make the work of others as good and effective as it can possibly be. And I've served for years as dean of a faculty, and that's what a dean does too. And I've been able to walk with my adult children in more supportive ways. This work of lifting up and supporting has brought me much joy.

And finally, I have come to know the essentiality of the quality of mercy. It's not an easy thing to learn. In my observation and experience, there are two ways to learn it—and pretty much only two. One learns it when one is denied mercy in a desperate hour. And one learns it when one receives mercy in a desperate hour. Sometimes we get to learn it both ways.

As Jenny did. Long after her ordeal, she told us that during the rawest, most hurting days, someone had directed her to a woman in another city who had a "gift of mercy." Jenny had showed up at her house, and the woman, after patiently drawing out her story for an hour and more, had taken Jenny back to a bedroom and tucked her ever so gently into the big bed. "Jesus is here for you now," she said softly. "He wants to gather you the way a hen gathers her chicks, like a shepherd gathers his lambs. He never gets tired of drawing us into his gentle embrace." She stroked Jenny's hair and prayed silently for her a good while until she fell asleep. Jenny said she slept for a long, long time. Mercy in a desperate hour.

Over these years I have come to know what a godly thing mercy is. And how rare. And what it feels like to be at someone's mercy and to be cast out. I've observed that, most often, only when we have been treated with a glaring lack of mercy can we truly recognize mercy when it is poured on us. When it is—and we know it—we desire to pour mercy over others.

I've determined—so help me God—to err on the side of mercy.

"Lord have mercy, Christ have mercy, Lord have mercy on me."

CHAPTER 24

WHERE THE BEAUTY CAME FROM

> "The sweetest thing in all my life has been the longing—to reach the Mountain, to find the place where all the beauty came from."
>
> —C. S. Lewis

At age eleven classical music started it all for me. My parents, wanting to divert me from what they viewed as the corrupting rock 'n' roll of the sixties, got me a set of LPs introducing the great composers: Bach, Mozart, Beethoven, Handel, Chopin, Strauss, Tchaikovsky, and a few others. I listened to them over and over during my early teenage years. I came to love them, to know them by heart. I got a taste of how beauty works, how it settles down deep in the soul, stirring feelings both noble and aching and giving glimpses into regions unknown.

Maybe this all started the day when my fifth-grade class got to go to the symphony orchestra. We were loaded onto a school bus, given sack lunches, and driven to the civic center and concert hall in Orlando. We joined hundreds of other elementary school children, finding our seats, watching the orchestra warming up on stage amid the buzz of voices. We had been instructed on some things about an orchestra: what it was, the various instruments, the kinds of music it played, the role of the conductor and the concert master. We were to applaud when the conductor entered and when an entire piece (not just a movement) was finished.

The orchestra played a whole Beethoven symphony and Prokofiev's *Peter and the Wolf*. My eyes could not move fast enough and my ears were not skilled enough to take it all in, but it was both fascinating and magical, glorious and mesmerizing. Unforgettable. What was this thing I had experienced?

For Holly a similar breakthrough happened—suddenly—at age nineteen when she stood in front of Michelangelo's *Pieta* in Rome and found herself overwhelmed. Spellbound. In exquisitely hewn marble, she beheld Mary's ineffably sad face cradling her beloved, lifeless son. And it wasn't just the inherent beauty of the sculpture. She experienced something deep and true there, and the encounter forever transformed her view of the role of beauty—of art—in her faith.

Philosopher Roger Scruton, in *Beauty: A Very Short Introduction*, wrote: "Beauty is an ultimate value—something that we pursue for its own sake, and for the pursuit of which no further reason need be given. Beauty should therefore be compared to truth and goodness, one member of a trio of ultimate values which justify our rational inclinations." This trio—the true, the good, and the beautiful—are traditionally known as the "three transcendentals." They were called that because they were viewed as the three qualities God possesses in infinite abundance.

A great theologian of our time spent much of his career seeking to reclaim beauty as one of the great transcendentals. In a world where sin and error are rife and truth and goodness hotly contested, beauty has a key role. Beauty, he says, can sail under the radar of our arguments over what is true and good and in the process smuggle in a ray of the beatific vision. Beauty can pierce the heart, wounding us with the transcendent glory of God. Beauty, he says, "dances as an uncontained splendor around the double constellation of the true and the good and their inseparable relation to one another."

Concerned about the neglect of beauty by Christians in our time, writer and poet Dana Gioia spoke of "the necessary relationship between truth and beauty, which is not mere social convention or cultural accident but an essential form of human knowledge—intuitive, holistic, and experiential." It is a form of human knowing that "awakens, enlarges, and refines our humanity."

Holly and I both grew up in a Christian tradition that highly valued truth and goodness but in which beauty had no intentional place—and certainly not as an "ultimate value" worthy of pursuit for its own sake. We would hear about the beauty of holiness. And the beauty of nature was to be praised because it was God's handiwork, but the accoutrements of man-made beauty were seen to easily distract the church from its God-given mission. The pursuit of beauty—as I learned in my childhood experience as well as in my historical research—was associated with refinement, excess, and wealth. Leaders like David Lipscomb (1831–1917) spoke sharply against elegant and expensive church buildings—and the well-to-do members who built them. The church, he believed, was "the especial legacy of God to the poor of the earth"; the rich—the usual patrons of the arts—tended to be the "great corrupters" of the church.

We also tended to read the Bible with a kind of flat-footed literalness that focused on facts and commands. In one of the most common formulations, the gospel was facts to be believed, commands to be obeyed, and promises to be enjoyed. In this way of reading, one must push past the "highly-colored imagery" in Scripture and retain only the "real facts and unadorned doctrine." The "poetic element" must be "rendered simple."

My parents embraced this traditional theology, which for them meant an indifference—sometimes even an aversion—to beautiful things. Everything about my childhood home was starkly and unexceptionally utilitarian. Simple, plain, inexpensive, bare. Sometimes ugly. Never any conversation about art, and, as far as I know, never any attention to music. Except hymns at church. (And a set of classical records for me—to protect me from rock 'n' roll.)

A vital part of my journey of faith has been a Christian theology of beauty. Here's how I've learned to put it: The beauty of God is the beauty of perfect love—the love between the Father, the Son, and the Spirit. The Incarnation of Jesus, with his dying and rising, becomes the clearest and most decisive portrayal of this love. We can call it a display of the "art" of God's love, so it becomes the supreme model of all worldly and human beauty. And the Holy Spirit—the one through whom God's love is poured into our hearts—becomes what we could call the "beautifier." The Spirit has befriended matter, befriended creation, and seeks creation's wholeness. Through the experience of created beauty, the Spirit awakens in us the desire for the wholeness, the *shalom*, of the age to come.

A Christian account of beauty is shaped not primarily by envisioning return to a paradise lost but rather anticipating a glory yet to appear—a glory or beauty already seen in Jesus Christ but that is being spread about through the Holy Spirit. The beauty we discern now is a preview, given by the Spirit, of a beauty yet to come in the new heaven and new earth. It is being revealed in the midst of a creation still groaning in anticipation (Rom. 8:20–22). Earth's most dazzling beauty is thus only a glimpse of the beauty to come.

C. S. Lewis, at the very end of the Narnia stories, put it like this: "All their life in this world and all their adventures in Narnia had only been the cover and the title page; now at last they were beginning Chapter One of the Great Story, which no one on earth has read; which goes on forever; in which every chapter is better than the one before."

A few years ago Holly and I attended a performance of Handel's *Messiah* by the Nashville Symphony and Chorus. It was conducted by the acclaimed maestro of the symphony, Giancarlo Guerrero, Nicaraguan born and a Baylor University graduate; he was joined by four acclaimed soloists and a 165-member choir. Guerrero directed without a baton, using his arms, hands, and all ten fingers as subtly and beautifully as any ballet dancer. It was magnificent.

I thought of Lewis's words: "We do not want merely to see beauty. . . . We want to be united with the beauty we see, to pass into it . . . to bathe in it." God placed a strong desire for beauty in every one of us, and this night at the symphony, I think the "beautifier" let us bathe in it.

There's the aria in Part 2 where the tenor sings, "Behold and see if there be any sorrow like unto his sorrow." In fifteen spare measures, Handel seems to catch up the anguish of the whole world. Or the final chorus, "Worthy is the lamb that was slain," which swells with grandeur and glory seldom matched in modern music. Who could not be moved? And not only moved. Caught up. Caught up in the God of beauty. Caught up in the Great Story, the story we believe to be the true story of the world.

Lewis again: "At present we are on the outside of the world, the wrong side of the door. . . . We cannot mingle with the splendours we see. But all the leaves of the New Testament are rustling with the rumour that it will not always be so."

CHAPTER 25

SPIRIT STORIES

> "The temptation to domesticate the Holy Spirit is almost irresistible."
> —Stanley Hauerwas

In my father's bookroom was a slim black volume titled *The Spirit and the Word* (1919) by a preacher named Z. T. Sweeney. Its subtitle didn't do much for me: *A Treatise on the Holy Spirit in the Light of a Rational Interpretation of the Word of Truth.* But I well remember this book. I certainly didn't read all of it, but here's what a curious eight- or nine-year-old boy got from it: since the late first century the Bible has replaced the Holy Spirit as God's means of working in the world.

Could that be true, I long wondered? It seemed unlikely, but what did I know? I suppose this long wondering helps explain why, for the last several decades, I've been telling Spirit stories. By that I don't mean stories focused on claims about the dramatic and mysterious intervention of the Holy Spirit. I mean, more simply, stories from the history of the Stone–Campbell Movement / Churches of Christ about how theologies of the Spirit took shape and played out. It soon became clear to me that the doctrine of the Spirit serves as a kind of litmus test for the theologies that shaped the tradition.

The first story has to be Cane Ridge. Perhaps as many as twenty thousand people gathered at Cane Ridge, Kentucky, in August 1801 for what would be called the Cane Ridge Revival. Hundreds were converted and perhaps a thousand experienced powerful manifestations of the Spirit in what has been called "America's Pentecost." Barton Stone's Presbyterian church was the host. A spirit of unity emerged among the Baptists, Methodists, Presbyterians, and others gathered there like Stone had never witnessed before. He attributed it to the Spirit's "fire." As a result, Stone envisioned a Spirit-empowered church, unconstricted by human creeds and unmindful of the fashions of the world. This powerful event provided the first burst of energy for Barton Stone's call to unite upon the Bible alone and to be "Christians only." Over the next decade Stone's "Christian" movement grew rapidly in the aura of Cane Ridge. It marked the modern-day beginnings of what began to be called the Church of Christ.

The second Spirit story I like to tell is about Alexander Campbell, whose "disciples" restoration movement emerged in the 1820s. Campbell was deeply put off by the aura of Cane Ridge; he called the theology of the revivals "the greatest delusion of this our age" and a prominent cause of the "irreligion of our contemporaries." In canvassing many thousands of pages in his periodicals, I calculated that he wrote over 1,600 pages on the Holy Spirit, much of it opposing the revival doctrine of the Spirit. He could say that, after the Bible was revealed, "all the power that could operate on the human mind is spent." Faith was "reason receiving testimony" from Scripture, not a result of any mysterious infusion of the Spirit. If Campbell was put off by the revival theology of the Spirit, I must say that I found myself put off by the Campbell theology of the Spirit. In the 1820s and 1830s Campbell's rational view of conversion spread throughout Stone's "Christian" movement, mostly eclipsing the aura of Cane Ridge and revivalism.

The third story has engaged me most of all. For a season in the 1990s I holed up in a borrowed cabin one or two days a week, week after week, to dig out the mostly untold story of four people in the 1850s. It was the story of Tolbert Fanning, Robert Richardson, the young Walter Scott Russell, and the old Alexander Campbell, plus a small cast of supporting characters. It was a poignant and illuminating story about the clash of two sharply opposed theologies of the Spirit. It unfolded in an intense written debate, resulting in deeply strained relationships, political fallout across the "brotherhood," a shocking departure, and a rare apology—as well as an eventual death on a Civil War battlefield.

After some hard searching and further poring over the literature, I finally found most of the missing pieces, and the story came together. It began with a polemical exchange in a series of articles by Richardson and Fanning published in Mr. Campbell's journal. Richardson believed—and had for many years—that a constricting philosophy had been allowed to intrude into the theology of the movement, shutting down a vibrant doctrine of the Holy Spirit and turning faith into little more than a rational transaction. Tolbert Fanning, at great length, denied the accusation and charged Richardson with heresy. At the end of the exchange, Campbell was pressed to take sides. And he sided with Fanning.

The result was estrangement between Dr. Richardson and his longtime and admired friend, Alexander Campbell. It told of the confusions, miscommunication, and hurts; of Richardson's sudden departure from Virginia and resettling in Kentucky; of the blackballing of Walt Russell, a brilliant young graduate of Bethany College who shared Richardson's concern but took it a step further. And then, after some time, an apology from Mr. Campbell to Dr. Richardson—something I had never seen from Campbell all the years before. Then, to my shock, there was Russell's death just a few years later at the Battle of Vicksburg (Mississippi), where he served as a chaplain. In all my work, I've seldom, if ever, been as moved and grieved as I was by this complex story.

In a book about the episode, I called it a (hidden) crossroads in the Stone–Campbell Movement—the place where two very different ways of construing the Christian life met, clashed, and diverged. One hundred fifty years later, the divergence is still playing out.

The doctrine of the Holy Spirit serves as a telling marker for the theologies that shaped the tradition. The theology of the Cane Ridge Revival gave way to the anti-revival theology of Alexander Campbell, which was then challenged in the 1850s by the classic theology of his friend Dr. Richardson, who embraced a God who draws near in intimate ways.

Richardson's strong theology of the Spirit was succeeded by that of James A. Harding (and a few others), who sounded similar notes. They believed that through experience of the Spirit our deep hunger for intimacy with God gets satisfied. But this theology was eclipsed in the early twentieth century by strong voices insisting that "no man today is influenced or led by the Holy Spirit." Yet the "Spirit question" would not go away. It emerged again in the 1960s as some began calling for a renewed emphasis on the empowering Spirit in the Christian life. And so it went—the doctrine of the Spirit continued to stir both controversy and hope.

I wanted to tell these stories not mainly because I loved historical detective work but because I had come to believe, as one of my deepest convictions, that our theologies are shaped—and how we practice our faith is shaped—more than we often know, by our traditions. That is to say, by where we have come from and who has influenced us. When we learn some of those stories, we can become more self-conscious; we can get loosened up, perhaps even freed up, for a richer and fuller embrace of Christian truth. Of course, one may also more readily distance oneself from the traditions. A good many do.

This conviction about the importance of locating ourselves, of getting a sense of where we've come from and the stories that have shaped us, has moved my work from the beginning. It's what I desperately needed to know as I came to young adulthood, and it's why I launched out on an extended expedition into the wilds of the Christian tradition. In one of my early books, I quoted F. J. A. Hort, a nineteenth-century Bible scholar, who said, "The air is thick with bastard traditions which carry us captive unawares while we seem to ourselves to be exercising our freedom and instinct for truth." And so it is we find ourselves in traditions propelled by the illusion of having none.

I'm still telling Spirit stories. The big story in recent times is that focus on and interest in the Spirit has risen to an all-time high in the history of the Christian faith. Not so much in the West, where the faith is contracting, but in the rest of the world where Christianity has been expanding at breakneck speed, mostly in Pentecostal/charismatic forms. This contrast has really captured my attention, and a few years ago I addressed it in a book, *Poured Out: The Spirit of God Empowering the Mission of God*. There I developed the doctrine of the Spirit in relation to God's mission in the world. And I pressed the point that when churches come alive to their mission in the world, the doctrine of the Spirit usually comes alive; and when churches get sleepy and settled, the doctrine of the Spirit usually recedes, becoming tame and doctrinaire.

But more than telling Spirit stories, I've been pursuing *life* in the Spirit through my own ups and downs, allowing myself to be drawn in by the Spirit of resurrection and joy. This Spirit has brought life out of deadness and gladness out of darkness and despair. The Spirit has turned my mourning into dancing.

CHAPTER 26

TO SET THE HEART RIGHT FIRST

> "Oh! To set the heart right first saves the head a world of useless trouble . . . ."
>
> —Robert Richardson

Over lunch some years ago, a new acquaintance asked me, "From all your reading and study in the history of the Stone–Campbell Movement, who have you appreciated and admired the most?" I didn't have to think twice. "It's Dr. Robert Richardson," I said. "No question."

My lunch partner, of course, wanted to know why. First, I explained who he was: a longtime younger colleague and friend of Alexander Campbell, the family physician, and, after Campbell's death in 1866, the one asked by the family to write his biography. Then I told him the reason for my appreciation. I've been asked this question many times over the years, and I always want enough time to well explain why.

To this inquirer, I said, "I admire Dr. Richardson's rich and graceful prose, which follows the elegant style of an earlier era.

But that's only a nice bonus. The basic reason he stands out to me is that, over many years, he pressed a vital theological corrective to the dominant direction of the movement." I explained that he heartily embraced Mr. Campbell's founding principles for restoring the ancient faith. But by the 1840s he had come to believe the movement was heading down a troublesome and counterproductive path—with Campbell himself leading the way. A corrective was needed because what Richardson called "a heartless and superficial formalism" was overtaking the movement. And this conviction only grew into the 1850s.

What Richardson called "formalism" is a common distortion of the Christian faith. Formalism sees Christianity as a new law, and its proponents tend "to substitute obedience for faith, [and] to exalt the precepts above the grace of God." It has a penchant for codification that always threatens to displace the biblical vision of faith as trust in and friendship with God.

I went on to explain Dr. Richardson's diagnosis and corrective. The problem was that trust in a living Savior was being eclipsed by a set of doctrines, faith was being "supplanted by polemics," and people were thereby growing distant from Christ. Richardson once wrote that too many Christians "are ready to argue, debate, discuss, at all times, and will spend hours in the earnest defense of their favorite theories," but will not spend five minutes meditating "upon the character, the sayings, the perfections of Christ, or upon their own inward spiritual state."

Some years earlier he had written a small book summarizing the basic principles of Mr. Campbell's reform movement—a volume that Campbell had commended. One of the most basic foundational principles of the movement, he had said, was a proper distinction between "the Christian faith" and "doctrinal knowledge."

Doctrine provided a necessary scaffolding for faith, but "a syllabus of doctrine has no power to enlist the heart and the energies of the soul in the true work of Christ." Christian faith centers on a person, not a body of doctrines; on a way of life, not a code.

For Richardson, faith at its heart is nothing more or less than "a trusting in Jesus, a personal reliance." He noted that when Jesus commended people for their faith, it was "because with a very moderate amount of evidence, there was exhibited a ready and confiding trust." Faith involves some knowledge or evidence, but it arises primarily out of the heart's "affections."

The central challenge is the setting of the heart's affections. The way of divine wisdom is "to correct the errors of reason by regulating the affections. . . . Oh! To set the heart right first saves the head a world of useless trouble," he exclaimed, "for it is truly through the heart alone that anyone can comprehend the 'doctrine of God.'"

The main source of the problem Richardson saw in the movement was the deep—often hidden—theological assumption that God could influence human beings only through revealed words and not in any personal and direct way. By the 1850s Richardson was alarmed that some influential leaders were dissolving the Spirit into the Word, claiming that the Spirit does not work in any way apart from the Word. One was left only with the biblical "facts." They were received through the eyes and ears into the mind as truth. This was the fullness of Christian life. There was nothing more. In this view, faith does not require that one have a relationship with the author, but only that the reader accept what the Word says as true.

The effect of this restriction was, Richardson thought, to "unfit men's minds to receive anything that is not merely outward and formal." The effect was spiritual debilitation and a fixation on outward forms. The effect was to squeeze the life out of the doctrine of the Holy Spirit. Such a theory denied any place for an encounter with God or for an actual sharing of the divine life. This was the key problem for Richardson.

Richardson insisted that the Bible and the Spirit work deeply together. Without the Word we do not know who God is, but without the Spirit we do not know God as a living presence in our lives. Both the Word and the Spirit are essential.

In Robert Richardson I found an eloquent voice, rooted deeply in the Christian theological tradition, that could speak of divine relationality, of real communion with God, and of our participation in the life of God. His work was a place I could start from to address a glaring deficiency in the tradition, which was the lack of a central and functioning doctrine of the Trinity.

Richardson himself did not develop an explicit focus on the Trinity. But his work points toward and helps set the stage for a more fully developed Trinitarian theology. It does this by recovering a vibrant doctrine of the Spirit and showing how that enables us to "participate in the divine nature" (2 Pet. 1:4). I found in Richardson's theology the most biblically rich focus on divine relationality I had seen anywhere in the heritage of Churches of Christ.

The antidote to "formalism" is a centering focus on relationship with God. And the foundational doctrine of the Trinity keeps that focus front and center.

In the New Testament we see a divine community perfectly united in self-giving love. When we use the shorthand word *Trinity*, we are catching up—summarizing—central biblical themes about God: God's relational nature seen all through Scripture; the love that binds Father, Spirit, and Son into a unity; God's movement toward us in the story of salvation; and the way we can be drawn into relationship with God and partake of God's life.

What if the Christian life, at its heart, is a pathway of participation in the life of the Trinity? What if the Father's love for the Son is the same love God has for us as adopted daughters and sons? And what if the Spirit of God pours that very love freely into our hearts, as we are able and willing to receive it? What if the Christian life involves beholding the beauty of the Lord—a beauty most visible to us in Christ—and reflecting some of this beauty back before the brokenness and ugliness of the world?

Here I found some of the answers I was seeking when in my early teens I set out on this long journey of discovery. What I found has revolutionized my understanding of what it means to be a follower of Christ.

CHAPTER 27

TRAVELS WITH PUDDLEGLUM

> "Puddleglum, desperately gathering all his strength, walked over to the fire. Then he did a very brave thing. . . . With his bare foot he stamped on the fire, grinding a large part of it into ashes on the flat hearth."
>
> —C. S. Lewis, *The Chronicles of Narnia*

My acquaintance with David Lipscomb began with my childhood forays into my father's bookroom, where I learned to find my way around in his big book *Questions Answered*. It answered some of my questions then. Though not the big ones. It did help me at least begin to understand the impetus behind some of my father's convictions and way of life.

My father had separated himself in striking ways from the ways of the world. He didn't talk politics—or even seem to care about such things. He didn't vote. He believed he was a citizen of God's kingdom first and foremost, not any earthly kingdom. He believed God ruled God's kingdom quite well and was not threatened by opposing powers. He believed wealth inherently corrupted the church and that God's people must live simply and with minimal regard for worldly fashion. And he believed that racial segregation was wrong—a glaring and ongoing sin among disciples of Jesus.

These convictions, I began to learn, had all been advocated by David Lipscomb three generations earlier. His contemporaries observed that he "lives in utter disregard of the notions of the world." He believed that the way of Jesus was "adapted to the common people" and that "the rich corrupt it," perverting it to fit their own tastes. "The great weakness of the church today," he wrote in 1889, "is that the children of God enter into the kingdoms of this world, imbibe the spirit of those kingdoms, bring that spirit into the church of God, defile the church and drive out the spirit of Christ." So he counseled Christians to maintain their primary allegiance to God's kingdom by refusing to get caught up in the kingdoms of this world—including not becoming combatants in the military, and even not to vote or to serve as postmasters.

And Lipscomb thought it was sinful to have two separate congregations in the same community for two separate races. "Nothing is more clearly taught in the Bible," he wrote in 1878, "than that Christ came into the world to break down middle walls, family prejudices, natural animosities, race antipathies, and to unite the different kindreds, tongues and tribes into one undivided and indivisible brotherhood."

I imbibed this outlook from my father and mother, of course. And as I traveled the road of theological discovery throughout my early adult years, some of these deep understandings went with me. But I didn't quite know what to do with Lipscomb. So I mostly just moved on—he was a strong voice in my heritage whom I would, perhaps, come back to one day. Churches of Christ themselves by the mid-twentieth century—caught up in the patriotic fervor of two world wars—had mostly rejected Lipscomb's more radical stance toward politics, war, and US culture. And they had long embraced the status quo of racial segregation. When World War II broke out, some patriotic members of Churches of Christ, not surprisingly, wrote that Lipscomb's book advocating these things—*Civil Government*—should be gathered up and burned.

Both Lipscomb and my parents viewed themselves as "resident aliens," members of an outpost of heaven. This image has deep roots in the New Testament: God's people are "foreigners and strangers on earth" with a "citizenship in heaven" (Heb. 11:13; 1 Pet. 2:11; Phil. 3:20). As an early Christian writer put it in response to the questions of an outsider: for us "any foreign country is a homeland, and any homeland a foreign country." Over the years of my work as a professor and theologian, these themes remained near the forefront.

When I began to work my way back to David Lipscomb after a good many years, it struck me that Lipscomb was a kind of Puddleglum figure. Puddleglum, as readers of C. S. Lewis may recall, is a strange character in *The Chronicles of Narnia*. He is a Marsh-wiggle who is gloomy and pessimistic and has large webbed feet. The children call him a "wet blanket" because he always expects the worst.

The witch-queen of the Underland has set a bonfire releasing intoxicating fumes by which she seeks to enchant and overpower the children, Eustace and Jill. Puddleglum has come to love the children. He realizes what is happening and with his webbed feet stomps on the blaze producing the magic smoke. Due to the stench of his burning flesh—"burnt Marsh-wiggle is not at all an enchanting smell"—and reduction of the enchanting smoke, the children come to their senses and escape the sorceress.

David Lipscomb reminded me of Puddleglum. Lipscomb believed the way of the world is characterized by a range of deceit, lies, and illusions. Or in the parlance of the apostle Paul, "The god of this age has blinded the minds of unbelievers, so that they cannot see the light of the gospel that displays the glory of Christ" (2 Cor. 4:4). Lipscomb believed the church itself in the culture around him had been enchanted, indeed often overcome by the magic smoke. And so he called the church to rouse itself. He wanted to clear the air, jolt Christians awake, and enable them to see the new world God has opened up in Scripture. To polite society (including many Christians living comfortably at home in "Christian" America), Lipscomb's alarms seemed exaggerated, cantankerous, sometimes heretical. Not to mention gauche and embarrassing.

It should be no surprise to learn that we have some contemporary Puddleglums. One is Stanley Hauerwas (1940–), longtime professor of theology and ethics at Duke University and author of many books. Notable ones include *Resident Aliens: Life in the Christian Colony* (1989) and *A Community of Character: Toward a Constructive Christian Social Ethic* (1981). In 2001 *Time* magazine acclaimed him on its cover as America's best theologian. Imagine that—a modern-day Puddleglum on *Time*'s cover!

I first met professor Hauerwas at a small gathering of theologians in 1993, where we had a good long conversation one afternoon while waiting for dinner. He asked me about my Church of Christ-related university, told me his (unexpurgated) opinion of Reinhold Niebuhr and of a Bible professor from my university who had departed years before to teach at Yale. Then several years ago he was on our campus for three days and I spent some hours with him. He was warm and engaging and very open in the classroom with our seminary students. He even appeared as a guest on Lee Camp's well-known *Tokens Show* (now called *No Small Endeavor* on National Public Radio), where Lee interviewed him. I still have a vivid image of Stanley swaying and clapping to the music with the other guests on stage.

Dr. Hauerwas was shaped by the Free Church trajectory of dissent against the ways of Christendom—as was David Lipscomb. And he is—like Lipscomb—a steadfast critic of theological liberalism, believing that the way of Jesus, rather than calling us to accommodate modern culture, puts us in sharp tension with some liberal ideals of the larger culture.

Hauerwas writes again and again that "the first task of the church is to be the church." What he means is that the very first priority of the church is to realize that it is not the world, that it lives by a very different story. This does not mean being anti-world. Rather it's an attempt to show the world what it is meant to live as God's good creation. The church must remember its story and live out its story. That is its first priority. Otherwise, it becomes disoriented and gets lost in the same smoky haze that blinds the world to God's story.

When I eventually circled back to David Lipscomb, I realized he was saying pretty much the same thing—though he lived in a different time, used much simpler language, and spoke to a very different audience.

So the church must be a distinctive and set-apart community, practicing an "alternative politics." In following the way of the cross, the church cannot help but appear odd and out of sync with the world. "We want to claim the church's oddness as essential to its faithfulness," Hauerwas wrote. A key part of this oddness is the conviction about who rules this world. "We would like a church that again asserts that God, not nations, rules the world, that the boundaries of God's kingdom transcend those of Caesar, and that the main political task of the church is the formation of a people who see clearly the cost of discipleship and are willing to pay the price."

David Lipscomb could have written these words. He did, in fact, write a good many like them.

When Christians begin to live and think as if they are at home in the world, something central to the faith has been undermined or lost. So the eschatological vision of the New Testament is crucial for the mission. In the power of the Spirit, God's kingdom is breaking in. The church by faith knows and experiences this. So it can live boldly and compassionately as "strangers and exiles" in the world.

So Hauerwas. So Lipscomb. Puddleglums both.

Another Puddleglum I traveled with some over the years was the British missionary theologian Lesslie Newbigin (1909–98). He spent thirty years in India then, upon his return to England, spent his remaining years writing several influential books, among them *Foolishness to the Greeks: The Gospel and Western Culture* (1988) and *The Gospel in a Pluralist Society* (1989). He is often viewed as the theological father of the missional church movement.

Newbigin argued that modern Western culture has been a powerful opposing force to the gospel over the last couple of centuries. The gospel has been exploding throughout the non-Western world for decades, he noted, but in modern Western culture it is "everywhere in retreat." Western churches have become compromised, assimilated, and timid. Newbigin's conclusion: the West has become—and needs to be approached as—a mission field.

Who would say such things to a *Christian* West and a *Christian* America? Puddleglum, of course.

I've traveled a good bit over the years with Puddleglum. Some may even think I've become one myself. But I don't think so. I lack the audacity, probably the courage. But I do happen to think that the times still call for a Marsh-wiggle with the clarity and courage to stomp his big webbed feet on the enchanting fire.

CHAPTER 28

MORE THAN IT SEEMS

> "The mystery of the church is that it is,
> by God's good grace, more than it seems to be.
> The Holy Spirit is the 'more' of the church."
> —Stanley Hauerwas and William Willimon

Another volume I found in the bookroom helped me further understand the Christian world of my childhood. It was a smaller book titled *The Church, the Falling Away, and the Restoration*, written by a late nineteenth- / early twentieth-century Church of Christ leader named J. W. Shepherd. I was a little older—ten or eleven—when I opened this book. It helped fill out the backstory for some of the basics I had already learned: that we had "no creed but the Bible," that we were not a denomination, and that we were nothing but New Testament Christians.

I didn't read the whole book, but enough to get a clear picture of the fall and restoration. It went something like this: the corruption of the church began early, even in the first century; it picked up speed as a hierarchy began to emerge; it adopted "inventions of men"—creeds and such; and within a few centuries the apostasy was complete. Darkness prevailed. The church of the New Testament was lost.

The first little sparks of reform broke out in the darkness of the fourteenth century with John Wycliffe and a few others, and then in the sixteenth century the light spread in the reforms of Luther, Calvin, and other Protestants. They recovered the Bible in the vernacular so people could read it for themselves. They spread some light, but they did not restore the church of the New Testament. The Protestant churches were not true churches because they all had "a human name, a human creed, and human practices." Their legacy was denominationalism.

The restoration of the New Testament church occurred in the early nineteenth century. Human creeds were put away as restoration leaders determined to "speak where the Scriptures speak and to be silent where the Scriptures are silent." On this basis, a full return to the New Testament was accomplished.

This historical narrative of apostasy and restoration made sense to me as a boy. It helped explain our separateness and distinctiveness. And it gave a sense of momentousness to our modest congregation in Winter Garden, Florida.

As my big questions began to emerge over the next few years, this narrative became one of the things that troubled me. I suspected that the story—the history—was more complex than that. Turned out it was.

It usually doesn't take a very long trek into the Christian past to be convinced that it's a pretty human and messy business. Indeed, one may become so keenly aware of the humanness of it all—one's own tradition as well as the others—that one is tempted to reject it. To brush it all aside and seek a new and untainted place. To nourish the dream of starting all over again.

That's what restorationists often sought to do. Just skip the mess of it all. Start back at the beginning. Shortcut around the muddy stream and go straight back to the pure spring, back to the untraditioned Scriptures. This impulse took different forms in different periods, as we have seen. Supporting it, in whatever form, was usually a "fall" narrative.

But this narrative had some problems. Over the early years of my trek into the Christian past, I began rethinking it. To claim that the church fell into complete or near-complete apostasy from the fourth century (or earlier) until the sixteenth or nineteenth century poses a serious problem—even if one posits a tiny, mostly untraceable remnant of the true church. Christ promised to build his church and preserve it against "the gates of Hades" (Matt. 16:18), which means the church is in God's keeping.

What we need to say is that Christ's church through all the centuries has been marked by strengths and by serious failings, by sacrificial faith and sometimes serious apostasy. There have been periods of decisive decline. Times of corruption and compromise with the world. Times when its light has been dimmed. It has waxed and waned. But even in its waxing it has remained blemished, populated and led by shortsighted and sinful human beings.

The classic Protestant slogan highlights the earthly character of the not-yet-glorified church: *the church reformed, yet always in need of being reformed.* This means that traditions make wrong turns and get off course. It means that "the present church, like the New Testament community of disciples, is often errant or fallen, often restored."

But God's church is more than that. It is more than it seems.

A well-known voice among Churches of Christ in the last decade of the nineteenth century was a man named F. D. Srygley

(1856–1900). He was the author of that odd volume, *Larimore and His Boys*, which I first saw in the bookroom when I was eight. Srygley wrote regularly in Lipscomb's magazine about being nondenominational. In a collection of those writings published after his too-short life, he said, "No church is at any time wholly free from apostasy. The mystery of iniquity is continually working in all churches. That God does bear with evil doers and continue to recognize a church as a church of Christ after it has committed some very grave errors, the Bible clearly teaches." However, churches can go beyond the limits of divine forbearance, he pointed out. "But the exact point at which it ceases to be a church of Christ no man can tell."

An unusual admission in the literature of Churches of Christ.

At Jesus's baptism the Spirit came to rest upon his body. The Spirit remained upon him and accompanied him all through the course of his ministry, all the way through his death, and was at work in his resurrection and exaltation. The Spirit continues to rest on bodies. Now it is Christ's body called church. The Spirit—as with Jesus—imparts strength for God's redeeming and reconciling work. Resting upon Christ's body, the Spirit enables witness to the new age dawning in Christ, always pointing to Christ, enabling people to confess that "Jesus is Lord."

We can hardly fail to miss the often sordid reality of the church through time—and in our own time. It's easy to assume—and many in our time do—that the church is just another human institution. It can be explained and accounted for by the usual social forces that we study and try to measure. It's pretty much like any other caring institution—only maybe it cares somewhat more.

But the church is more than it seems. More than a good caring society. The Holy Spirit is the more. Because the Spirit has come to rest on the church, the church is the embodiment of redemption and an alternative to the kingdoms of this world. The Spirit animates, gives life to the church. The Spirit makes the church possible—the visible, warts-and-all church.

Here's one way it works. In every age God raises up "new movements of protest, witness, and fellowship." These independent churches tend to be "socially unbalanced, theologically unbalanced, and poor, . . . but meanwhile they are out being the Church." They are unsophisticated, often uneducated and ill-equipped. And our world today—especially the Global South—is full of them. But they are much more than they seem to be. The Holy Spirit is the more.

In Scripture the purposes of God are always focused on an actual community. Three big concepts in Scripture carry this focus: Israel, kingdom, and church. They are all expressions of God's covenant community. Kingdom is always, in its largest expression, the realm in which God's will is being established and practiced. And the church is a local expression of God's kingdom, a very concrete here-and-now community. To become—and remain—a Christian is always to be incorporated into Christ (by baptism) and thereby into his visible and local body.

The people of God are a gathered people, called out from every tribe, nation, and tongue to be a new nation, a peculiar people. The call to worship (in the traditional liturgy) gathers this new people in its local setting. We are called out and assembled to be constituted into the end-time community, part of that "great multitude . . . from every nation, tribe, people and language, standing before the throne and before the Lamb" (Rev. 7:9). On the Lord's Day we join with that "great multitude," declaring, in advance of the final reality, that we are joining with the one people of God.

Holly and I have been members of about twelve congregations over the course of our lives. Rural and suburban. Small town and big city. Traditional and innovative. Ones with mostly older members and with mostly young members. In all of them, we found many people, as I said about the members of my boyhood church, who were steadfast, committed, gracious, often sacrificial, showing up week after week, year after year, to teach the Bible, serve the needy, embrace the hurting, encourage one another, and seek to honor God. Ordinary saints. Some more ordinary than others. A scattering of hypocrites. Some troublemakers. Many strugglers. Sinners all. People of faith on whom the Spirit has come to rest, making up churches that are more than they seem to be.

The church's high calling is to share in the mission of the triune God, where the grace of Christ through the power of the Spirit is breaking down walls of separation and forming "one new humanity" (Eph. 2:15). The church in every place falls sadly short of this high calling. But it is actually much more than it seems. The Holy Spirit is the more.

CHAPTER 29

THE LONG JOURNEY

> "What one encounters in a retrieval of the Tradition is the recognition that Christianity is far richer than one's own personal and ecclesiastical experiences."
>
> —Daniel H. Williams

The questions, as I said at the beginning, began in my preadolescent years. And these questions were the beginning of my long journey. So strong and persistent were the questions that eventually I set aside the medical career I had been intending and took up theological pursuits. The answers I sought were somewhat slow in coming. But I did find them over the course of the years.

As I look back, my body of work, in outline, has had four main dimensions. First was a focus on Alexander Campbell's nineteenth-century "restoration movement" as a function of its time and place—the way it was shaped (and limited) by its cultural context in profound ways. This kind of historical work was what I was after in my doctoral training, and I sought to apply it to my own heritage. So I underscored that, though Mr. Campbell made an heroic effort to throw off all tradition, he remained shaped profoundly by it: by the Presbyterian tradition in which he was reared, by the Scottish intellectual tradition in which he was schooled, and by the young American tradition of democratic individualism in which he lived. My writings in this dimension include *Things Unseen: Churches of Christ in (and After) the Modern Age* (2004), which pulled together research and writings from the previous two decades.

Second was extending the story of the restoration impulse back through time in order to set Churches of Christ beside other restoration movements, comparing their different emphases and agendas. If Mr. Campbell and his heirs focused on the "ancient gospel" and "ancient order of things," other restorers—Anabaptists and Pentecostals, for example—focused on authentic discipleship of Jesus or on life in the Spirit. The comparisons were telling and instructive. My work in this dimension includes *Discovering Our Roots: The Ancestry of Churches of Christ* (with Richard Hughes, 1988) and "The Restoring Impulse in the Great Stream," in *In the Great Stream* (2021).

Third was exploration of the theology of Churches of Christ—the doctrine of the Trinity, for example, and the Holy Spirit—and pressing for corrective and enrichment. The tradition never placed much focus on—or reached any consensus about—the doctrine of the Trinity. Trinitarian language was optional at best. And regarding the Spirit, the tradition tended to embrace a thin and rationalistic doctrine out of step with the Great Tradition. These were serious theological problems that I sought to address and amend. My writings in this dimension include *Participating in God's Life: Two Crossroads for Churches of Christ* (with Danny Swick, 2003) and *Poured Out: The Spirit of God Empowering the Mission of God* (2018).

Fourth was seeking to situate Churches of Christ in the Great Tradition for the purpose of becoming more strongly anchored in the foundational truths of early Christian orthodoxy. This included situating Churches of Christ on the big map of Christian history, highlighting the particular stream—the Free Churches—in which they were constituted. And it included critiquing the rejection of tradition that tended to put Scripture at the interpretive whim of the lone individual. My work in this dimension includes *In the Great Stream: Imagining Churches of Christ in the Christian Tradition* (2021).

A few things about where I've come out on this journey. A steady theme running through my work over the years is that we are all part of thick traditions that are deeply rooted in times and places. This means we are contingent creatures. Contingent means "dependent on or conditioned by something else." It means shaped, often in unconscious ways, by time and place. Contingency is a feature of God's good ordering of creation. God made us dependent and culturally embedded creatures. It also means we are considerably beset by limitations, brokenness, misjudgment, and other assorted maladies. And furthermore, it means the faith does not come to us in generic and disembodied form—simply as a set of ideas or a system of truths. It comes to us in this or that living tradition embodied in these people here or those people there. People whose names we often know.

So my journey necessarily took me back into the thick tradition that formed me. Early on, this tradition deeply impressed on me that, unlike the various denominations around us, our church was the one Jesus founded. Heroically freed from the captivity to tradition, it was simply the New Testament church. Baptized at age eleven, I was grateful to be a member of the true church. But by age thirteen and before, I began to sense there was more to the story than I had been told. I had been told—and readily assumed—that it came simply from the Bible. I needed to see where it came from and the influences that shaped it. So through nine years of seminary and doctoral work, I traveled a winding path of discovery. Several of my stories have portrayed parts of that journey.

Many of us at some point launch out from the parochial Christian world in which we grew up toward a larger world that beckons. If we become students of the broader Christian tradition, we soon discover that the Christian heritage is longer, richer, and more variegated than we ever dreamed. It is populated with saints and martyrs and eloquent preachers and bold missionaries, along with opportunists, counterfeits, and not a few rascals. We soon find ourselves awash in the wonder and messiness of it all. Immersed in all of this, we may at times experience a measure of doubt about the very possibility of "clean" and solid truth. Over the last four decades I've noticed that the journey of doctoral students in Christian history and theology often arcs through disorientation and disenchantment, sometimes cynicism and disengagement. That path can be deadly to vibrant faith.

I've experienced these temptations and hazards, felt the disorientation, the relativizing pressures. Doctoral work in theology seems designed to make that happen. Things long taken for granted get challenged and unsettled, sometimes deconstructed. Such an attitude easily becomes a habit, a reflex. But deconstruction is not—should not be—the endgame. I remember Flannery O'Connor's advice to "Push back against the age as hard as it pushes against you." The age—*this* age—has its own deep-seated, often hidden assumptions about reality, its own shifting and faddish orthodoxies. We learn to push back against them, to critique the critical theories, to relativize the reigning ideologies.

Through all of this, I can say, my faith has become broader, deeper, and stronger. I've found a solid and soul-sustaining place in what we can call classic Christianity. It is sometimes called the Great Tradition. It is anchored and symbolized by the Nicene Creed. To be a Nicene Christian is to be rooted in the world of ancient and orthodox faith of the first four centuries. It is to embrace Scripture as the supreme resource enabling a consistent vision of God and the order of creation, with the incarnate and exalted Christ as the focus. It is to trust the Spirit's work through the church fathers and mothers, and to set one's anchor in the core doctrines set out in the Nicene settlement. It is to be tutored in the way of Jesus by apostles, saints, martyrs, and exegetes. All this formed the base of the Great Tradition. It is the richest, weightiest, and most anchored place I know.

But isn't this Great Tradition flawed? Of course. As it was curated over the many centuries, it sometimes took wrong turns. It sometimes made unholy alliances and compromises. It sometimes oppressed the recalcitrant and endorsed the world's ethnic and racial prejudices. It could sanction empire and wars in the name of the Christian West or East. Precisely for this reason, the restoring impulse, with its heightened sense that the tradition makes wrong turns and can get off course, has played an important role. Restorers prod and provoke the church to take notice. They shake up and challenge the comfortable and the compromised. They gravitate toward the common folk and tend to discount respectability, sophistication, and status. Of course, the restorers too are flawed, shortsighted. They too get blindsided by their own time and place—witness, for one example, the ready embrace of racial segregation over the last two centuries. The Great Tradition and the long restorationist tradition each need the other.

The Stone–Campbell Movement / Churches of Christ sought to break with the Great Tradition, to leap over it and make it mostly irrelevant. It didn't want the baggage. It didn't want the burden of tradition. It wanted only the untraditioned Bible. But the reality is that the Bible is always traditioned to us. Its message is always handed on—filtered, we might say—through ongoing communities (traditions) of readers who want us to be blessed by Scripture as they have been. And in a time like ours, when truth has become light and balloon-like and when many attempt to make up their own orthodoxy, we need the anchoring weight of the Great Tradition.

Churches of Christ comprise a real, live tradition. It has been a tradition carrying forward the central claim to be free of human tradition. The tradition was shaped and carried forward by human beings. Contingent human beings. When we miss this reality, two things tend to happen: we become blind to the (unacknowledged) tradition, and we tend to absolutize it, turning it into a kind of idol. The strength of the restoration vision, properly understood, helps us with these two tendencies. It helps shine fresh light upon Scripture. It awakens us. It helps us to keep testing—in light of our human contingency—the faithfulness of our theological construals, our interpretive decisions, and our discipleship practices.

I venture the opinion that it will be difficult for any particular Christian tradition—including Churches of Christ—to stand strong in the face of the mounting pressures of secularism in our time unless it goes deep into its own tradition, and not only its own tradition, but deep into the much larger and longer Christian tradition—the Great Tradition. I believe that if it does go deep, it will thrive in character and substance, though perhaps not in sheer numbers.

Every church has to decide what it considers basic and essential beliefs. The list can be long or short. Who decides? Someone or some group or some tradition does in fact decide. That's what Christians were forced to do in the early centuries. In the face of many challenges and threats to the faith, and through a Spirit-led collective discernment, church leaders—pastors, bishops, theologians, and evangelists—decided what constituted, to use C. S. Lewis's term, "mere Christianity." (He was using "mere" in its older meaning: pure, unalloyed, undiluted.) They held up a specific set of beliefs and practices judged to be faithful and necessary features of the apostolic Tradition. This became the Great Tradition.

This vista emerged as the destination of my long journey of faith.

CHAPTER 30

A BRIDGE TO SOMEWHERE

> "The first task of church history as a theological discipline is to free Christians from their own parochialism and make them truly catholic."
>
> —David Steinmetz

In early 2014 a conversation with my wife, Holly, left me with a helpful metaphor to describe the nature of my theological journey over the last three decades or so. I was pondering this journey because my publisher had proposed a twentieth-fifth anniversary edition of *The Cruciform Church*, which was to include response essays from several people and a new conclusion by me. At about the same time I was asked to speak to a group of church leaders on the topic "*The Cruciform Church*: Twenty-Five Years Later." I was trying to get a handle on what had changed—and how I'd changed—over this quarter century.

So I asked her, "How would you characterize what has happened over these decades with this book and the others that preceded it?"

"I've had an image in mind for a long time," she said. "It's the image of a bridge. We grew up on an island. A pretty small and remote island. We knew there was a mainland out there—a larger, expansive place. But we weren't sure how to get there. So you've been trying to build a bridge. A bridge that would connect the island with the mainland. That's at least how I picture it."

"I like that image. Say a little more about it."

"Okay. You, along with several colleagues who preceded you, thought it was a good thing, maybe a necessary thing, to engage and explore life on the mainland. So you threw yourself into bridge building. It seemed perilous at times. Some thought it threatening, dangerous. Some thought it would be a bridge to nowhere. But turned out it became a passable bridge that has connected us to to the mainland with its rich gifts."

"It's coming back to me. You've spoken of this bridge before, right?"

"I have. In our desert season years ago. You were at your lowest, almost unable to see any future. In a letter I said that God had used you to help construct bridges for people. And that many had happily crossed over to a freer place in Christ. A place that has blessed them in their continuing spiritual journeys both on the island and on the mainland. Though you seemed unable to travel there yourself."

"I remember now. That time in the desert and these years since have made a big difference for me. I've crossed the bridge. Finally. And I am able to travel both ways, sharing the gifts from our island and receiving the gifts of the mainland."

In my speech to the church leaders a couple of months later, I used her image. I said:

When the first three books appeared in 1988 followed by *The Cruciform Church* in 1990 and *Distant Voices* in 1993, there was a surprising explosion of interest. In the years since, thousands of church members have told me how refreshed and broadened they were by these books. And I still hear it, almost every week.

Readers often spoke of finding words for the gnawing difficulties they had long experienced with their Christian heritage. "So much of what you wrote," said one letter, "gave justification to the feelings I have wrestled with for years. I have struggled since my childhood with both the spiritual wealth and poverty of my heritage, but in this struggle I lacked understanding of why. Your efforts in this book helped answer a great deal of the why." Another said, "Your book surprised me, but in a good way. I had no idea about the long history of the restoration vision. I began to see how the age, the particular context, shaped the focus. I thought—of course it would. Seeing a larger horizon has enriched and clarified the present for me."

As I've continued to hear from these readers, I've realized what those books provided. They helped form a kind of bridge. A bridge from the island connecting it to a broader Christian mainland.

The bridge, of course, is a metaphor. A way of capturing an opening up to the larger body of Christ. How does this opening up happen?

One important way is through a deepening sense of Christian history. The sense of that history complicates our present. It makes it harder to be simplistic about our convictions and where we came from. Makes it harder to remain comfortably ensconced on one small, isolated island. Careful historical work forces us to face the reality that we are limited and dependent creatures, and broken—which is to say human. "Careful historians know just how richly complicated, contradictory, and varied are the ways human beings understand what they do and what they think." They help us begin to see how formed we are by our time and place, by traditions and influences that we do not—and will never—fully grasp. In this way, the sense of history jostles and challenges our easy parochialism and opens up a larger horizon.

Over these decades I've traveled far and wide beyond the island and come to have deep appreciation for the richness and variety of far-flung Christian places. And on those travels I have marveled at the way the faith—the gospel about the incarnate Christ—has made its way deeply into a vast range of tongues, tribes, and nations. At the way the gospel itself becomes incarnated in cultures, including my own Southern US subculture. And how most everybody's church is the product of a "labored tradition," which means not that each one is equally right and true, but that each one has "its own integrity and deserves a respectful hearing."

I've traveled far and found brothers and sisters all over. But the island has remained my homeplace. It's a place well-known and loved, a place whose ways are ingrained as habits in me. And it's a place upholding a good many of the basic convictions that matter to me.

In my lifetime, however, the island has become much less remote and cut off—maybe even no longer an actual island. It is now linked to the mainland by a well-traveled causeway, or—perhaps a better image—by an isthmus, a sizeable piece of solid land. The promise of this new accessibility is not that we can now join up with so-called Mainline Christianity on the "mainland"; the Mainline Churches decades ago lost their way and have been in steep decline ever since. Rather, the mainland is a place where we can find our bearings in the long, deep, and rich tradition of the church—the "communion of saints," past, present, and future.

The challenge to the church now is not so much to guard and shelter remote island life with its distinct dialect and tradition. Rather, the challenge to the church is a new kind of secularism that is pressing on Christian faith as a whole in the West. One philosopher calls this new secularism life in the "immanent frame." In the immanent frame the very awareness of and openness to divine transcendence—to an unseen spiritual realm—diminishes. Firm and settled beliefs are steadily buffeted by fierce "cross pressures" that make truth seem flimsy and unstable. In this frame "the presumption of unbelief has become dominant" in numerous spheres of life, especially the academic sphere. So it may not surprise us that thirty million people in North America who used to call themselves Christian have now deconverted—become "nonverts."

To what degree do we seek to accommodate the new secular order and to what degree resist? In a time like this, many of us who were formed in very conservative Christian traditions—that is, on various islands—and have made our way to the mainland will likely be drawn in one of two basic directions. Some will seek to play catch-up to the dominant culture of the mainland, to get in step with the modern moral order, and to travel a path toward some variety of progressive faith. And some will attempt to push back harder against the accommodationist posture and move toward a faith anchored solidly in classic Christianity—the Great Tradition. These aren't the only two options, of course, but they seem most likely for former island dwellers.

I have chosen the second option. This is my bridge to somewhere.

CHAPTER 31

THE GOOD LEFT OVER

> "That there's a little of the good
> left over from a few lives
> is a comfort of sorts."
> —Wendell Berry

My mother was a letter writer. During some of my hardest times, mainly during the college years, her letters flowed. Always handwritten. Always encouraging. Almost always long. They were marked by steadfast confidence in God, insights from her life experience, and reminders of the daily attending to the necessary details of life. And of course advice on good nutrition.

Early in my college years, she wrote: "Follow Jesus hard, and cling to God's Word. The teachings are rich and true, and the promises are trustworthy in every aspect of our lives." And in my junior year, just prior to my wedding, she admonished: "Live with a good conscience every waking hour. Don't forget this! Life is too short and eternity too long to 'toy' with life." Such letters continued over the years that followed.

When dementia slowly began to set in twenty-five years ago, I missed the letters. I missed her fun-loving spirit, her teasing, her full presence. Even her nutritional advice.

But there was plenty, plenty of the good left over.

My father's legacy was a different matter. I had never received, as far as I could tell, his blessing. He had been aloof from much of what I cared about. At his passing I had been almost indifferent. Over the years since I had not much missed him. At his memorial service I had shared, with appreciation, what I viewed as his legacy to me: care for language, for faith, and for good health. Yes, I could be thankful for that.

But quite a few years later I came to see that I had more to attend to. I remembered a couple of lines from the contemporary poet Dana Gioia:

> What we conceal
> Is always more than what we dare confide.
> Think of the letters that we write our dead.

I had not written many letters to my father in the several years before he died—and certainly none since then. But maybe it was time. One afternoon I began. I tried to say things I had never been able to say during his life. Some things I didn't know I needed to say. Some I hadn't wanted to say. As I wrote, to my surprise, tears began rolling down my face, and they didn't stop until well after I had finished writing.

Here's a condensed version of the letter:

> Dear Dad,
>
> Your boy needed you all those years in Winter Garden. I wanted to know more of who you were. I wanted you to

see me. I wanted you to do things with me, to take some interest in my creative projects. I wanted you to watch me play basketball. I wanted you to be proud of me.

And when I grew up and spent many years studying the Christian faith—a faith you had instilled deeply in me—I wished you at least had been curious about my studies and asked what my journey was like, asked to read some of my writings. I never said any of these things to you. I guess I didn't know how. I'm sorry. I think we both need forgiveness.

Your son

"Remembrance is necessary, but so, too, is forgiveness." Over these many years I *have* remembered. It has been with sadness, regret, disappointment, sometimes amusement, sometimes indifference. But now I am beginning to remember with forgiveness. And from that newer and clearer perspective, the past is getting reconfigured, even redeemed. I have come to perceive a good bit more of the good left over.

Recently, Holly and I celebrated our fiftieth wedding anniversary. We held a reception at our church on a Sunday afternoon. Our three children and families were present, along with most of our extended family from around the country, as well as many friends from near and far. We wanted the occasion to be a testimony, especially for younger couples, to the possibility of enduring commitment. Holly and I each shared some reflections.

She wouldn't let me see the notes for her remarks beforehand. I soon learned why. She began by mentioning her original wedding surprise. Then she said she was going to surprise me again—yes, with the song she sang walking down the aisle fifty years earlier. Right there, at the reception, she sang the whole song—again:

> I come to offer my love to you,
> yours to have and cherish your whole life through.
> Deeper than the deepest ocean
> is the depth of my devotion,
> And so I bring all my love to you.
>
> My arms will carry you through the day;
> my lips will pray with you when you pray.
> Both my hands will lift you higher;
> this will be my heart's desire,
> And so I bring all my love to you.
>
> In sorrow, in sadness,
> in joy or care,
> You need never fear tomorrow,
> for I'll always be there.
>
> And God who causes the sun to shine,
> when he made you,
> made you to be just mine.
> So he smiled down from above you,
> called this heart of mine to love you,
> And so I bring all my love to you.

Once again—now fifty years later—I barely held it together. It's a sentimental song, but no matter; it was our song—certified and sealed over fifty years.

After the song, Holly spent a few minutes touching on the different seasons of our life together. "We've had fifty years together," she concluded, "forty-five of them really good. [laughter] It's been a privilege and joy to love and honor Leonard all these years."

The first half of our marriage focused on my career. The second half focused on hers. In my remarks, I told the reception guests how, over these last twenty-five years, it was my turn to be a sounding board for her ideas and a reader of her speeches and chapters and book manuscripts. And it was my turn to be the primary cook. Most evenings, I would have a hot meal prepared when she came in the door from the university. And her response was almost always the same delighted response: "My favorite!"

The launching pad for her new career had been something she experienced at an innovative church we were part of for a few years. She witnessed the impact of different generations brought intentionally together in a church community. It stirred an unquenchable question: What was this, and why did it seem so powerful? That question drove her PhD research. It drove her to write *Intergenerational Christian Formation* (IVP, 2012/2023), which has become a widely used seminary textbook. It drove her to envision and begin an international conference called InterGenerate (2017, 2019, 2021, 2023).

To Holly's great surprise, she became a leading international authority on intergenerationality in Christian churches. She calls it an unexpected career that began with a burning question she could not stop pursuing. Over these years I've received lots of warmth and light from the fires she has been building and tending. I learned more about all things intergenerational than I ever knew there was to learn. It's been my privilege to journey alongside her, support her, lend her my editorial experience—and cook for her.

Through the ups and downs of my life, I have come to love her more deeply and to love her well. This increased ability, best I can tell, results from two things: the growth of my character as a more steadfast, open, and unselfish person; and the fact that we have sought to secure our love in "the eternal," that is, in God's love that transcends our own egos.

In the midst of our darkest and most overwhelming time—the long desert season—we made a firm commitment to each other. We said: "We want to learn everything possible from this—we don't want any of the pain to be wasted. We want it to change us, to grow us, and to temper us. We want always to forgive each other. We want to use all of this for something good. And we want to finish well."

I will be so bold as to say that by God's grace—and by fits and starts—we have been doing this with and for each other over these many years since. And looking back through it all, we continue to discover more of the good left over.

I think the traditions of faith that have shaped us so powerfully work somewhat the same way. We have not yet fully explored them and indeed will never be able to, but we seek to attend to them and understand as much as we can. In the remembering, we find good and strong things that have formed and enriched us. And in the remembering, we invariably face the need to forgive those who have gone before. And as we forgive, we become able—so I have found—to discern and receive more of the good left over.

The truth is that our pasts are marked by brokenness—in our families, our close relationships, our congregations, and our complex traditions. We carry the memory of wrongs—wrongs done *against* us and wrongs done *by* us. What shall we do with those memories? Shall we seek simply to block them out? Is that even possible? Or shall we seek to hold onto the painful memories as a strong safeguard against further wrongs? No.

I believe that as we step into God's forgiveness and as we grow in our capacity to accept and enjoy God's love, the memories of wrongs—both our own and those done against us—will diminish in their weight and in their power to haunt us with hurt or guilt. Perhaps we can sometimes even not remember or not call to mind some of the wrongs, though I submit that is possible only as a weak human echo of God's forgiveness—a God, Scripture says, who does not remember our sins (Jer. 31:34; Heb. 8:12, 10:17).

Our past is broken, but we do not—cannot—discard it or leave it behind. It is vital to who we are. "God does not take away our past; God gives it back to us—fragments gathered, stories reconfigured, selves truly redeemed, people forever reconciled."

In that regathering we will find access to a good bit more of the good left over.

AFTERWORD

> "The writer operates at a peculiar crossroads where time and place and eternity somehow meet. His problem is to find that location."
>
> —Flannery O'Connor

Two or three mornings most weeks I head out early to a coffee shop for a couple of hours to read and write. It's usually my "secret" coffee shop, an out-of-the-way place that people from my world do not frequent. Since I came to coffee so late, you understand, I still have some catching up to do. The baristas are mostly college students and young songwriters who all know my name—and who often have my freshly ground coffee almost ready by the time I get over to the counter. Most weeks a young man from the neighborhood comes in with his two large goldendoodle dogs, Henry and Teddy, which I greet and pet until they settle down. No ashes to go—yet—at this shop. But a pastor has a small congregation meeting in the building, and he has offered me his little office whenever I want a quieter place.

This small shop suits me—as such a place has for the past twenty years or so. It's a good place to remember, to make sense of things. A good place to reflect on the nourishing fruit of forgiveness. And a good place to let realities settle and hopes rise.

By now I think I can say that "Simple English" has become my mother tongue. At least I know well how to work for it. The blank computer screen—formerly the blank sheet of paper—does not freeze me up. And the fifth draft or the tenth—it's all part of the process. And the ear is pretty well-tuned to the sound of words. Though I am not really a poet.

My aspirations have been, oddly, both grand and modest. I might have aspired to write for a broad range of Christians in general. But a host of writers and scholars have been doing that with rich effect in these decades. I chose—at least I think it was a choice—to write mostly for one particular tradition, addressing the often hidden realities of their (our) story, and seeking to enrich it by connecting it to the larger Christian story—to build a bridge from the island. It has required an intimate knowledge of the island and good familiarity with the expansive geography of the mainland. I've sought to find, as Flannery O'Connor put it, that unique crossroads where time and place and eternity intersect.

It all began with the big questions from my childhood, which first took shape around my father's dinner table and in his bookroom. I can truly say that I found good—or at least satisfactory—answers to those questions. The trouble is that those answers have had an uncanny way of stirring up new questions. And that's the way it should be, I think, in a God-created world full of wonder, and mystery, and brokenness, and touches of grandeur all around. A world of marred beauty, restless groaning, and sacraments of divine grace.

Well along in my journey now, I have a strong and clear sense of where I am. I'm no longer baffled, chagrined, or distressed by the deep cultural particularities—the embeddedness—in which we all find ourselves as Christians. It's how the gospel, as a reflection of the Incarnation, spreads. It gets "translated" deep into the heart of every culture in which it is received. My journey of many years has taken me from the cultural confines of a nineteenth- and twentieth-century restoration movement in the United States into the deep and true heart of the Christian faith—Trinity, Incarnation, and life in the Spirit.

It's been a long journey, driven by pressing questions.

Along the way, I have worked at remembrance . . . of hard things, good things, forgotten things. I've come through a long season in the desert, a deeply transformative time. I have worked to forgive and to receive forgiveness, a continuing grace. I've made progress on the inviting slopes of the second mountain, and now . . .

Now I find myself more firmly anchored in the faith, more alive in the Spirit, and more at peace than at any other time in my life. I've learned to dance, yes. But I've gained something else—a most unexpected gift.

I would call it something not unlike a father's blessing, but received only after a long and roundabout detour. Best I can tell, it is God the Father's grace and love mediated to me by actual human beings, men in the flesh. Three in particular. Each one, to my great surprise, sought me out—in the desert—and gave me a gift when I did not know how to seek or even for what. Three gifts from three very different people, given over a season of years.

I have come to see now that their very different gifts, received together, have made up something close to what fathers do for their sons and daughters: let them see into their father's heart, give them sturdy love and approval, share with them his wisdom about how the world works, and model for them an honest, gracious, and disciplined life.

The very writing of these stories has brought these gifts into focus. The giving and the receiving of them makes up a deep feature of my story—one of the Spirit's welcome surprises.

In this long season, as I've grown in my own understanding and experience of a father's blessing, I have been seeking to bless my adult children. In my sometimes faltering way, I try to embody the characteristics above: (1) let them see into my heart—the love I have for them and for Holly, the vulnerabilities I sometimes feel, even the fears I wrestle with; (2) give them sturdy love and approval—tell them often that I love them, and say, almost every time I am with one of them, "I am proud of you"; (3) share my wisdom about how the world works—I try to be careful here, sharing my insight and advice mostly when I am asked for it; and (4) model before them an open, gracious, and disciplined life—a life of respect, forgiveness, and steadfastness. If these practices can make up something close to a father's blessing, then I can say with a modest measure of confidence that they are being blessed.

The bookroom remains a fixture in my memory. In the early years it yielded some important secrets about my father and the pathway he first set me on. But the books are long gone (except for a handful my mother left me). A few of the sermon notes and prayers are in a storage box somewhere. I revisit the room sometimes in my mind, but I don't stay long. I am mostly at peace with it.

And once in a while, I think back to mealtime around my father's table all those years ago. The conversations around it shaped me in ways I still don't fully understand. But that's not my table any more. There's no more Tiger's Milk for me; instead, it's the table of fellowship around which I relish the gifts of food and friends, of bread and brotherhood, of laughter and love. And around the table of the Lord, it's the encounter with the invisible but real presence of Jesus, who is real food and real drink—a taste of life in fellowship with the Trinity.

REFERENCES

Opening epigraph: Wilfred McClay, "The Claims of Memory," *First Things*, January 2022, https://www.firstthings.com/article/2022/01/the-claims-of-memory.

Preface

"They numbered approximately": Carl H. Royster, *Churches of Christ in the United States: Includes All 50 States and the Territories* (Nashville: 21st Century Christian, 2016), electronic edition.

Chapter 1

Epigraph: Eugene F. Rogers Jr., *After the Spirit: A Constructive Pneumatology from Sources Outside the Modern West* (Grand Rapids: Eerdmans, 2005), 13.

Chapter 2

Epigraph: McClay, "The Claims of Memory."

"five books on the history and theology of Churches of Christ": C. Leonard Allen, Richard T. Hughes, and Michael R. Weed, *The Worldly Church: A Call for Biblical Renewal* (Abilene, TX: Abilene Christian University Press, 1988); C. Leonard Allen and Richard T. Hughes, *Discovering Our Roots: The Ancestry of Churches of Christ* (Abilene, TX: Abilene Christian University Press, 1988); Richard T. Hughes and C. Leonard Allen, *Illusions of Innocence: Protestant Primitivism in America, 1630–1875* (Chicago: University of Chicago Press, 1988); C. Leonard Allen, *The Cruciform Church: Becoming a Cross-Shaped People in a Secular World* (Abilene, TX: Abilene Christian University Press, 1990); and C. Leonard Allen, *Distant Voices: Discovering a Forgotten Past for a Changing Church* (Abilene, TX: Abilene Christian University Press, 1993).

Chapter 4

Epigraph: Cynthia Ozick, *Metaphor & Memory: Essays* (New York: Knopf, 1989).

Chapter 5

Epigraph: Umberto Eco, *Foucault's Pendulum* (New York: Harcourt, 1989).

"not any 'friends'": C. S. Lewis, *The Four Loves* (1960; reprint, Boston: Mariner Books, 1971).

Chapter 6

Epigraph: Edgar A. Guest, "The Good Little Boy," *When Day Is Done* (Chicago: Reilly & Lee, 1921).

Chapter 7

Epigraph: Enid Nemy, "Adelle Davis: 67 and Going Strong," *New York Times*, June 14, 1971, https://www.nytimes.com/1971/06/14/archives/adelle-davis-67-and-going-strong.html.

Chapter 8

Epigraph: John R. Howard, "Identification of the Church of Christ," *Christian Magazine* 1 (1848): 267.

As a medical website put it: "Comfrey," Mount Sinai, accessed December 20, 2023, https://www.mountsinai.org/health-library/herb/comfrey#:~:text=Comfrey%20ointments%20have%20been%20used,and%20can%20lead%20to%20death.

Opinion of creeds: David Lipscomb and E. G. Sewell, *Questions Answered*, ed. M. C. Kurfees (Nashville: Gospel Advocate, 1921), 109.

Campbell's view of creeds: Alexander Campbell, *A Debate between Rev. A. Campbell and N. L. Rice, on the Action, Subject, Design and Administrator of Christian Baptism; also, . . . on the Expediency and Tendency of Ecclesiastic Creeds* (Lexington, KY: A. T. Skillman & Son, 1844), 784.

Chapter 9

Epigraph: David Lipscomb, "The Cholera and the Christian Religion," *Gospel Advocate* 15, no. 28 (July 17, 1873): 650.

View of denominations: Lipscomb and Sewell, *Questions Answered*, 175–76.

"to enter the kingdom, sinners": Lipscomb and Sewell, *Questions Answered*, 108.

Chapter 10

Epigraph: Mitch Albom, *For One More Day* (New York: Hachette, 2008).

"silent on the subject of race": Wes Crawford, *Shattering the Illusion: How African American Churches of Christ Moved from Segregation to Independence* (Abilene, TX: Abilene Christian University Press, 2013), 109–17.

"We do not believe that segregation": Reuel Lemmons, "The Church and Integration," *Firm Foundations* 81 (March 31, 1964): 194.

Chapter 11

Epigraph: Thomas Merton, *The Seven Story Mountain* (New York: Harcourt Brace, 1948).

Chapter 13

Epigraph: Jacques Barzun, *Teacher in America* (Boston: Little, Brown and Company, 1944), 48.

"Do you think I could be a writer?": Annie Dillard, *The Writing Life* (New York: HarperCollins, 1989), 70.

"Always read what you have written aloud": David Bentley Hart, "How to Write English Prose," *The Lamp* blog, January 2023, https://thelampmagazine.com/blog/how-to-write-english-prose.

Chapter 14

Epigraph: Nicholas Wolterstorff, *Lament for a Son* (Grand Rapids: Eerdmans, 1987).

Chapter 15

Epigraph: Jaroslav Pelikan, *The Christian Tradition: The Emergence of the Catholic Tradition (100–600)* (Chicago: University of Chicago Press, 1975), 2.

a magisterial five-volume work: Jaroslav Pelikan, *The Christian Tradition*, 5 vols. (Chicago: University of Chicago Press, 1975–89).

Chapter 16

Epigraph: Wendell Berry, *Standing by Words: Essays* (Berkeley: Counterpoint, 2011), 14.

One of a trio: The other authors were Richard T. Hughes and Michael R. Weed.

Moses Lard wrote in 1863: Moses Lard, "Do the Unimmersed Commune?," *Lard's Quarterly* 1 (Sept. 1863): 44, 49.

A late nineteenth-century leader: Austin McGary, "Rebaptism," *Gospel Advocate* (May 28, 1884): 338.

Campbell . . . as early as 1837: Alexander Campbell, "Any Christians Among Protestant Parties," *Millennial Harbinger* new series, no. 1 (Sept. 1837): 411–13.

Chapter 17

Epigraph: Robert Benson, *Digging In: Tending to Life in Your Own Backyard* (Colorado Springs: WaterBrook, 2007).

Chapter 18

Epigraph: Miriam Toews, *A Complicated Kindness* (New York: Knopf, 2004).

Chapter 19

Epigraph: W. H. Auden, "In Memory of W. B. Yeats," *Another Time* (New York: Random House, 1940).

Chapter 20

Epigraph: Miriam Toews, *Swing Low: A Life* (New York: Harper, 2011).

A three-step process: David Brooks, *The Second Mountain: The Quest for a Moral Life* (New York: Random House, 2020).

Chapter 21

Epigraph: Leonard Cohen, "Dance Me to the End of Love," track 1 on *Various Positions*, Columbia, 1983.

"The life of the Trinity": Diogenes Allen, *The Path of Perfect Love* (Boston: Cowley, 1992), 52.

"grace is not gentle": Kathleen Norris, *Amazing Grace: A Vocabulary of Faith* (New York: Riverhead, 1999), 151.

Chapter 22

Starbucks chain numbers: "Number of Starbucks stores worldwide from 2003 to 2022," statista, https://www.statista.com/statistics/266465/number-of-starbucks-stores-worldwide/.

Chapter 23

Book on spiritual abuse: Ken Blue, *Healing Spiritual Abuse: How to Break Free from Bad Church Experiences* (Westmont, IL: InterVarsity Press, 1993).

"we have to start from woundedness": Dallas Willard, *Renovation of the Heart: Putting on the Character of Christ* (Carol Stream, IL: NavPress, 2002), chapter 11.

"what a godly thing mercy is": The language in this paragraph is adapted from Holly Allen's chapel speech, "Lord, Have Mercy," January 2010, John Brown University, Siloam Springs, Arkansas.

Chapter 24

Epigraph: C. S. Lewis, *Till We Have Faces* (London: Geoffrey Bles, 1956).

"Beauty is an ultimate value": Roger Scruton, *Beauty: A Very Short Introduction* (Oxford: Oxford University Press, 2011).

"Beauty can pierce the heart": Hans Urs von Balthasar, *The Glory of the Lord: A Theological Aesthetics* (San Francisco: Ignatius Press, 1982).

Poet Dana Gioia: Dana Gioia, "The Catholic Writer Today," *First Things*, December 2013, https://www.firstthings.com/article/2013/12/the-catholic-writer-today.

"the especial legacy": Anthony Dunnavant, "David Lipscomb on the Church and the Poor," *Restoration Quarterly* 33 (1991): 75–85.

"highly-colored imagery": James S. Lamar, *The Organon of Scripture* (Philadelphia: J. B. Lippincott & Co., 1860), 235.

"All their life in this world": C. S. Lewis, *The Last Battle* (London: The Bodley Head, 1956), chapter 15.

"We do not want merely to see beauty": C. S. Lewis, *The Weight of Glory and Other Addresses* (New York: MacMillan, 1949), 12–13.

"on the outside of the world": C. S. Lewis, *The Weight of Glory*.

Chapter 25

Epigraph: Stanley Hauerwas, "How to Be Caught by the Holy Spirit," *ABC*, November 14, 2013, https://www.abc.net.au/religion/how-to-be-caught-by-the-holy-spirit/10099524.

Cane Ridge: Leonard Allen and Carisse Berryhill, eds., *Answered by Fire: The Cane Ridge Revival Reconsidered* (Abilene, TX: Abilene Christian University Press, 2020).

"the theology of the revivals": Alexander Campbell, "Mr. Lynd on the Influence of the Holy Spirit," *Millennial Harbinger* new series, no. 1 (Sept. 1837): 410; Campbell, "Dialogue on the Holy Spirit—Part 1," *Millennial Harbinger* (July 1831): 295–96; Campbell, "Incidents on a Tour to Nashville, TN—No. 1," *Millennial Harbinger* (Dec. 1830): 560; Campbell, "Kindgom of Satan—No. 2," *Millennial Harbinger* new series, no. 2 (Feb. 1838): 70.

"In a book about the episode": C. Leonard Allen and Danny Gray Swick, *Participating in God's Life: Two Crossroads for Churches of Christ* (Abilene, TX: Leafwood Publishers, 2001).

"no man today is influenced or led by the Holy Spirit": J. C. Holloway, *Christian Leader and the Way* (May 1905): 1.

"the air is thick with bastard traditions": F. J. A. Hort, *The Way, the Truth, and the Life* (1893; reprint, Cambridge, UK: Cambridge University Press, 2010), 91.

Chapter 26

Epigraph: Robert Richardson, "Nature of the Christian Doctrine—No. 1," *Millennial Harbinger* 4th series, no. 6 (Apr. 1856): 204.

"Formalism": Kenneth Kirk, *The Vision of God: The Christian Doctrine of the Summum Bonum* (1931; reprint, Cambridge, UK: James Clarke, 1990), 137.

"basic principles of Campbell's reform movement": Robert Richardson, *Principles of the Reformation*, ed. Carson Reed (1853; reprint, Orange, CA: New Leaf Books, 2002). The short quotes in this and the next two paragraphs come from this work.

"To correct the errors of reason": Richardson, "Nature of the Christian Doctrine—No. 1."

"unfit men's minds": Robert Richardson, "Faith vs Philosophy—No. 5," *Millennial Harbinger* (1857): 329.

Chapter 27

Epigraph: C. S. Lewis, *The Silver Chair* (London: Geoffrey Bles, 1953), chapter 12.

"the great weakness of the church today": David Lipscomb, *Civil Government: Its Origin, Mission, and Destiny, and the Christian's Relation to It* (Nashville: Gospel Advocate, 1889).

"Nothing is more clearly taught in the Bible": David Lipscomb, "Race Prejudice," *Gospel Advocate* (Feb. 1878): 120–21.

"an early Christian writer": *Epistle to Diognetus* 5.5.

Stanley Hauerwas: John Shelton, "Stanley Hauerwas: Modern American Puddleglum," Mere Orthodoxy, May 8, 2018, https://mereorthodoxy.com/stanley-hauerwas.

"the first task of the church": Stanley Hauerwas, *Resident Aliens: Life in the Christian Colony* (Nashville: Abingdon, 1989).

"a powerful opposing force": Lesslie Newbigin, *Living Hope in a Changing World* (London: Alpha International, 2003), 83; Michael Goheen, *The Church and Its Vocation: Leslie Newbigin's Missionary Ecclesiology* (Ada, MI: Baker Academic, 2018), 195–96.

Chapter 28

Epigraph: Stanley Hauerwas and William Willimon, *The Holy Spirit* (Nashville: Abingdon, 2015), 44.

"the present church": James McClendon, *Ethics: Systematic Theology*, vol. 1 (Nashville: Abingdon, 1986), 32.

"No church is at any time wholly free from apostasy": F. D. Srygley, *The New Testament Church* (Nashville: Gospel Advocate, 1910), 26.

"In every age God raises up 'new movements'": John Yoder, "Marginalia," *Concern for Christian Renewal* 15 (1967): 78.

Chapter 29

Epigraph: Daniel H. Williams, *Retrieving the Tradition and Renewing Evangelicalism: A Primer for Suspicious Protestants* (Grand Rapids: Eerdmans, 1999), 208.

"Flannery O'Connor's advice": Sally Fitzgerald, ed., *The Habit of Being: The Letters of Flannery O'Connor* (New York: Farrar, Straus and Giroux, 1979), 229.

"anchored by the Nicene Creed": For a brief exposition, see Phillip Cary, *The Nicene Creed: An Introduction* (Bellingham, WA: Lexham, 2023).

Chapter 30

Epigraph: David Steinmetz, *Taking the Long View: Christian Theology in Historical Perspective* (Oxford: Oxford University Press, 2011), 43.

"Careful historians know": Kathryn Lofton, "Why Religion Is Hard for Historians (and How It Can Be Easier)," *Modern American History* 3, no. 1 (2020): 69–86, doi:10.1017/mah.2019.26.

"the product of a 'labored tradition'": David Edwin Harrell Jr., "Epilogue," in *The American Quest for the Primitive Church*, ed. Richard T. Hughes (Champaign: University of Illinois Press, 1988), 243.

"life in the 'immanent frame'": Charles Taylor, *A Secular Age* (Cambridge, MA: Belknap Press, 2007), 542–56.

"the presumption of unbelief": Taylor, *A Secular Age*, 13.

"become 'nonverts'": Stephen Bullivent, *Nonverts: The Making of Ex-Christian America* (Oxford: Oxford University Press, 2022).

"drawn in one of two basic directions": Suggested by James K. A. Smith, *How (Not) to be Secular: Reading Charles Taylor* (Grand Rapids: Eerdmans, 2014), 138–39.

Chapter 31

Epigraph: Wendell Berry, "The Handing Down," *New Collected Poems* (Berkeley: Counterpoint, 2012), 46.

"What we conceal": Dana Gioia, "Unsaid," *Interrogations at Noon* (Minneapolis: Graywolf, 2001), 69.

"God does not take away our past": Miroslav Volf, *The End of Memory: Remembering Rightly in a Violent World* (2006; reprint, Grand Rapids: Eerdmans, 2021), 79.

Afterword

Epigraph: Flannery O'Connor, *Mystery and Manners: Occasional Prose* (New York: MacMillan, 1969), 59.

"translated deep": Lamin Sanneh, *Translating the Message: The Missionary Impact on Culture* (Maryknoll, NY: Orbis), 1989.

ACKNOWLEDGMENTS

I should first say that I never considered writing a memoir—even after my daughter Bethany made the request, on my birthday no less, for me to write stories about my life. Her request arrived complete with a schedule to follow. She is a gifted and accomplished writer and, being a journalist, used to working by deadlines. I wanted to honor her request, her gift. So I began to try my hand at some stories. She was my first reader.

There was no plan for a memoir at first. Just some episodes about my childhood and my father and my church. But to my unending surprise, after a few weeks of practice, I took to the regimen of story writing. As the stories began to flow, a vision and a plan emerged. And that's where my wife Holly became indispensable to the whole undertaking. She was my second reader. She gave me perspective and proportionality. When I thought I was going too far, saying too much, she sometimes said to go further, say more; and when I thought I was too understated and spare, she often said it sounded about right. She jogged my memory and filled in gaps. She talked me through the hardest times—times that easily get distorted in one's memory. She unearthed some key letters. She neutralized my doubts, and more than anyone thought these stories should see the light of day. The growing collection began to become a memoir.

To be clear: the writing of a memoir is a fraught undertaking. The pitfalls, the experts say, are many. One is the temptation to unleash a barrage of life details—most of which, no doubt, were significant for one's life but which, spread out over a raft of pages, quickly become tiresome, at least to those who are not members of one's immediate family. Another is a temptation to tell too much of other people's stories, peeking into their hidden places, divulging their failings, confessing their sins. There are more. There is the temptation to enlarge, exaggerate, and invent—to remember too big. And the opposite temptation: to downplay, smooth over, and scrub clean. And there are still more.

It's a wonder anyone writes a memoir and lets it go public. The fact that I have actually done that is only explainable—and defensible—by Bethany's bold request and Holly's clarity and steady assurance.

In addition to Bethany and Holly, a small troupe of people did their best to help me avoid the looming pitfalls of the genre. One was Dana Chamblee Carpenter, author of the popular novels that make up *The Bohemian Trilogy*. She provided a deep reading of the first full draft, which proved crucial to its final shaping. See knows memoir; she teaches memoir writing. To my delight, she really liked it. But she spoke her mind; she questioned the place of several stories; she asked for more. She said I needed a stronger "through-line" to bind it together. She was right. Her expertise made a significant difference.

There were a few others. Greg Taylor, longtime collaborator on book projects back in the early years of Leafwood Publishers, brought his keen writer's eye to bear on these stories near the end and helped make them better. And Jason Fikes of ACU Press understood what I was trying to do and gently pressed me to do it somewhat more, while Mary Hardegree blessed me with her strong editorial oversight.

My two sons, David and Daniel, who enliven a few of the stories, were gracious in giving their approval. And I would be remiss not to mention that Stanley Hauerwas, theologian extraordinaire and friend, heartily approved my making him a character in one of the stories.

To the three friends—you know who you are—who gave me the unexpected gift of friendship over these many years, I will simply say that I love and trust you forever.

Finally, to Holly, who has loved and supported me in ways I cannot fully fathom or number, this is for you most of all.

Leonard Allen
Advent 2023

BOOKS BY LEONARD ALLEN

The Worldly Church: A Call for Biblical Renewal, with Richard Hughes and Michael Weed (1988; expanded edition, 1991)

Discovering Our Roots: The Ancestry of Churches of Christ, with Richard Hughes (1988; Portuguese translation, 1990; Japanese translation, 1991; Korean translation, 2010)

Illusions of Innocence: Protestant Primitivism in America, 1630–1875, with Richard Hughes (1988)

The Cruciform Church: Becoming a Cross-Shaped People in a Secular World (1990; Korean translation, 1997; expanded edition, 2006; anniversary edition, 2016)

Distant Voices: Discovering a Forgotten Past for a Changing Church (1993)

Communings in the Sanctuary, by Robert Richardson; edited and introduced by Leonard Allen (2001)

The Transforming of a Tradition: Churches of Christ in the New Millennium, edited by Leonard Allen and Lynn Anderson (2001)

Participating in God's Life: Two Crossroads for Churches of Christ, with Danny Swick (2003)

The Contemporaries Meet the Classics on Prayer (2003)

Things Unseen: Churches of Christ in (and after) the Modern Age (2004)

Poured Out: The Spirit of God Empowering the Mission of God (2018; Korean translation, 2020)

Answered by Fire: The Cane Ridge Revival Reconsidered, edited by Leonard Allen and Carisse Berryhill (2020)

In the Great Stream: Imagining Churches of Christ in the Christian Tradition (2021; audiobook, 2023)

An Inspiring Voice, A Forward Call: Marshall Keeble Reconsidered, edited by Leonard Allen and Edward J. Robinson (forthcoming)

More Distant Voices: Discovering a Hidden Past for a Church on the Way (forthcoming)

C. Leonard Allen has taught Bible, theology, ethics, and philosophy at five universities and seminaries and has spoken widely at churches and colleges for four decades. He holds a PhD in History of Christian Thought from the University of Iowa School of Religion and is the author of several books (see the list on page 223). He directed a university press for almost a decade, where he oversaw the editing and publication of many books on Scripture, theology, church history, Christian living, and Christian higher education.

The central focus of his work has been opening up the riches of the Christian tradition across the ages to believers old and young. He also likes to grow sunflowers. Leonard is married to Holly, and they have three children and five grandchildren.